AFFILIATE MARKETER ON FIRE!

It's Not About
SELLING
It's All About
TELLING

---

*Special **FREE** Bonus Gift for You*

To help you to achieve more success, there are

FREE BONUS RESOURCES for you at:

https://FreeGiftsFromJoAnn.com

Surprise Guest will give you a jump start
in this video to help you get started today.

Using the Give First Model
God's Way

JO-ANN WOLLOFF

Copyright © 2022 AFFILIATE MARKETER ON FIRE, ALL RIGHTS RESERVED. No part of this book or its associated ancillary materials may be reproduced or transmitted in any form or by any means, electronic or mechanical, including photocopying, recording, or by any informational storage or retrieval system without permission from the publisher. PUBLISHED BY: JO-ANN WOLLOFF, OWNER BRIDGING THE DIGITAL GAP, DISCLAIMER AND/OR LEGAL NOTICES While all attempts have been made to verify information provided in this book and its ancillary materials, neither the author or publisher assumes any responsibility for errors, inaccuracies or omissions and is not responsible for any financial loss by customer in any manner. Any slights of people or organizations are unintentional. If advice concerning legal, financial, accounting, or related matters is needed, the services of a qualified professional should be sought. This book and its associated ancillary materials, including verbal and written training, is not intended for use as a source of legal, financial, or accounting advice. You should be aware of the various laws governing business transactions or other business practices in your geographical location. EARNINGS & INCOME DISCLAIMER With respect to the reliability, accuracy, timeliness, usefulness, adequacy, completeness, and/ or suitability of information provided in this book, JO-ANN WOLLOFF, BRIDGING THE DIGITAL GAP and its partners, associates, affiliates, consultants, and/or presenters make no warranties, guarantees, representations, or claims of any kind. Readers' results will vary depending on several factors. All claims or representations as to income earnings are not to be considered as average earnings. Testimonials are not representative. This book and all products and services are for educational and informational purposes only. Use caution and see the advice of qualified professionals. Check with your accountant, attorney, or professional advisor before acting on this or any information. You agree that Jo-Ann Wolloff, Bridging the Digital Gap is not responsible for the success or failure of your personal, business, health or financial decisions relating to any information presented by Jo-Ann Wolloff, Bridging the Digital Gap or company products/services. Earnings potential is entirely dependent on the efforts, skills, and application of the individual person. Any examples, stories, references, or case studies are for illustrative purposes only and should not be interpreted as testimonies and/or examples of what reader and/or consumers can generally expect from the information. No representation in any part of this information, materials and/or seminar training are guarantees or promises for actual performance. Any statements, strategies, concepts, techniques, exercises and ideas in the information, materials and/or seminar training offered are simply opinion or experience, and thus should not be misinterpreted as promises, typical results or guarantees (expressed or implied). The author and publisher (Jo-Ann Wolloff, Bridging the Digital Gap or representatives) shall in no way, under any circumstances, be held liable to any party (or third party) for any direct, indirect, punitive, special, incidental or other consequential damages arising directly or indirectly from any use of books, materials and or seminar trainings, which is provided "as is," and without warranties. Disclaimer

WHAT OTHERS ARE SAYING ABOUT
Jo-Ann Wolloff

"Jo-Ann Wolloff has hit affiliate marketing like a storm. Her insight into organic reach is refreshing. I Highly recommend her to get started or to see what you might have missed in affiliate marketing."

Kevin Harrington
CEO HBD Inc. Original Shark from Shark Tank

"If you're ready to positively transform your life, then read and absorb the strategies in this brilliant book by my friend JoAnn Wolloff! She truly cares about helping others and her ideas will make a positive difference in your life!"

James Malinchak
Featured on ABCs Hit TV Show, "Secret Millionaire"
(Viewed by 50 Million+ Worldwide)
Authored 25 Books, Delivered 3,000 Presentations & 2,000 Consultations
Best-Selling Author, Millionaire Success Secrets
Founder, www.BigMoneySpeaker.com

"This book is the secret weapon that every business owner or manager of a business can use as part of their overall marketing strategy. Jo-Ann Wolloff has put together a unique easy to follow success blueprint, to create passive and multiple income strategies right away. Her book and coaching is incredibly valuable in many ways for any business. 'Affiliate Marketer On Fire' is truly magical! Well done!"

John Formica
The "Ex-Disney Guy"
"America's Customer Experience Speaker, Trainer & Coach

"Jo-Ann Wolloff, as a speaker, coach and now best-selling author is making a splash. Her high energy and authentic nature are very contagious. Anyone would be lucky to learn from Jo-Ann."

- Patty Aubery - NY Times #1 Best Seller
"Chicken Soup ForThe Soul"

"Jo-Ann Wolloff has a unique way of getting her point across. You find yourself saying 'Why didn't I think of that?'". Jo-Ann is the real thing. "

Jill Lublin
International Speaker
4X best Selling Author & PR Expert

"JoAnn! I am so proud of you and thankful that you are BEING YOU!!! You are such a gift and you have found your place to serve others from your huge, overflowing heart!!! You are an amazing Coach!!! and you ARE making a difference!!! Keep it going, girl!"

Cynda Teachman Harris
GROW LIFE CoachingNetwork
https://www.growandflourish.com

"Jo-Ann is the best of the best when it comes to teaching others how to create multiple streams of income with affiliate marketing. Get ready to be on fire!

"You absolutely smashed it!! One of the best I've seen on these inspiration panels You ARE a speaker, and your authentic character came out and it was awesome! "

Nick Unsworth
https://www.lifeonfire.com

"Jo-Ann does an incredible job teaching you how to build and grow your business as an affiliate...it truly is a must read!"

Megan Unsworth
Queen of Coaching LOF
https://www.lifeonfire.com

"You are a wonderful person with the energy of a toddler, and I love it! You show up with a legacy of encouraging videos! JoAnn Wolloff you are one of those people that you come across in your life that you say to yourself "I will never forget her"

Gena Loutsis Peth

"Thank you, thank you, thank you!! Not just for your time and help with my page. I learn so much about navigating through funnels. I'm such a rookie. Your knowledge and skills are awesome. And for you to take time to help me and others shows your true character and integrity. I look forward to seeing your success. That alone is motivating. Knowing that this really works."

Randy Duerlinger

"Hey JoAnn, once again, I just wanted to tell you that I love your spirit, I love your enthusiasm and I love your helpful nature. All throughout Life on Fire experience you've been a positive light. finally read some of the articles in Live Abundantly and I just want to say I love the article you submitted to the book, I never knew you had to bounce back from so much in one summer, what a blessing teaching us to focus on the positive. Your "No one left behind" attitude is so awesome. Thank you."

Michelle E. Richards

"JoAnn you are awesome!! I admire your focus".

Ana Rutherford

"You're a riot. Just watching you do jumping jacks improves MY cardio. "The future's so bright, I gotta wear shades"

JD Dunphy

"You have been AMAZING! Whenever I get stuck and I can't figure it out, the first thing that comes to mind is, "What would JoAnn do?" This happened a lot more than the times I actually called you. "

Andre Grant

I just got this!!! – thanks JoAnn I've been trying to figure out affiliate marketing for t better part of this year I'm no idiot (I started my own boutique franchise law practice in '15) but it's been next to impossible for me to find the perfect elevator-summary of affiliate marketing.. UNTIL NOW! thanks entirely to you! You rock JoAnn, this is the perfect Godsend for me.

Brandon Garrett

"I could not be happier to see such a kind, compassionate & hardworking individual receiving acknowledgement for her work!! So, so, excited for you & inspired by you! JoAnn!! You are limitless!"
·Jacqueline S Barnes

You are such an encouragement! Contagious enthusiasm!!"
Randall Walters

"WOW! You are totally amazing. You continue to give in every way possible. I am so proud to call you, my mentor."
Kathi Goodwin

"I met JoAnn in the 1st week of joining a coaching academy. She immediately took me under her wing and what I loved was that instead of private message chats she would hop on a zoom call to talk in real time. I was so impressed at her desire to get right to the connecting. JoAnn celebrated and cheered me on every single step of the way and even gave me some of her behind the scenes "secrets" she was doing/implementing."
Danielle Pomerleau

"Can't say enough, your heart is in the right place and your words and life reflects"
LS Kirkpatrick

"Congratulations to our dear friend JoAnn Wolloff on the release of her book: Affiliate Marketer on Fire! JoAnn is the real deal. She went from being unexpectedly unemployed at the beginning of the pandemic to earning a great living as an affiliate marketer in less than a year and is now a nationally recognized expert in the process. She did it all with the heart of a servant and I firmly believe that's the secret to her success."
Chuck Vosburgh
VosburghandVosburgh.com

"You are an inspiration for me.".
Gerda Le Roux

"Such an inspiration, Jo Ann!!!"
Lalo Pacheco Sanchez

"JoAnn, You're amazing!!!"
Zelda Nera Hutzenbeler

"JoAnn Wolloff YOU are contagious"
Ana Isabel Placencia

"JoAnn you are amazing and genuine. What an inspiration you are."
Tonja DrPastor Williams

That is awesome. You work joyously hard and give beyond measure"
Vimala Richards

"Truth! JoAnn...as I watch your awesome video's, specifically about YOUR mentors, I am blown away at what and how you are in essence mirroring and paying it forward through the immense support YOU are doing and providing for us. I can excitedly and BOLDLY say and declare that unbeknownst to you, you have quickly become one of my mentors in business, and you and I are YET to even talk on a personal level!! It's simple: YOUR energy is through the roof and infectious! YOUR business and tech experiences and the desire and active way you move and inspire people to do the same is incredible! YOUR willingness to give back/pay it forward through your own support is amazing and humbling! Be and remain blessed"

Eva Bilungi

"JoAnn you are one of my greatest wins" The opportunity to spend 1:1 coaching time with you as you gently guide me in decision-making and goal-setting makes me want to hold myself accountable to not only myself but to others. I have learned to lead by example and do things "scared" at times. Thank you for your knowledge and insight into the world of technology. Together we will be stewards in Christ."

Sandra Wallace
The OCD Coach

MOTIVATE AND INSPIRE OTHERS!

"Share This Book"

Retail Price $17.97

5-20 Books	$15.97
21-99 Books	$13.97
100-499 Books	$11.97
1000+ Books	$9.97

To Place an Order Contact:

joann@bridgingthedigitalgap.com

THE IDEAL PROFESSIONAL SPEAKER FOR YOUR NEXT EVENT!

Any organization that wants to develop their people to become "extraordinary," needs to hire Jo-Ann Wolloff for a keynote and/or workshop training

JO-ANN WOLLOFF

EMAIL

joann@bridgingthedigitalgap.com

THE IDEAL COACH FOR YOU!

Any organization that wants to develop their people

If you're ready to overcome challenges, have major breakthroughs and achieve higher levels, then you will love having Jo-Ann Wolloff as your coach!

JO-ANN WOLLOFF

CONTACT

Jo-Ann Wolloff

EMAIL

joann@bridgingthedigitalgap.com

DEDICATION

It is with respect, admiration, sincere appreciation, and Love, that I dedicate this book to my mom and dad. Without you and the lessons you have taught me throughout my life and the unconditional love you gave me, I would not have the Blessing of being where I am today. Thank you for teaching me God and Family First.

Terry & Ray Thivierge

Here's What's Inside...

1. Everyone is an Affiliate........................1
    Mindset

2. Definition of Affiliate Marketer................6
    My Definition

    Internet Definition

    Action

    Affiliate Deals

3. Passive Income................................19
    Tell Don't Sell

    Affiliates' Questions

    Lessons

4. My Beginnings.................................35
    Which Courses?

    Groove

    Facebook Cover

5. Getting Your First Sales.......................64
    Second Sale

    Third Times A Charm

    All Set Right? WRONG!

6. What to Do Next..........................75
    Relationship Building

    Intentional Posting

7. Money Flow...............................99
    How did I make money?

    Facebook Covers

8. Is Experience Needed?..............105
    Don't Have to be Techy

    Photo Shoot

    Get a Tribe

    Groups

    Influencer

9. Accountability..........................126
    Always Celebrate Your Wins

10. Write A Book..........................143
    Ask For Help

    Products & Services

    Mentors

11. Mentioning Others...................158

Dear Friend,

My name is Jo-Ann Wolloff, and I am from a mill city called Woonsocket in the small state of RI.

I come from a normal size family for Woonsocket but fairly large for most other states.

Dad dropped out of school in 7th grade, mom left in 10th grade, both needed to work to help support their families.

They were married before they were both 20 years old and proceeded to have 8 kids in 9 years.

We were one of the poorest families in town, but I didn't know that till I was an adult.

I thought everyone shared their bedroom with 3 sisters and had 1 bathroom for 10 people.

Raymond, Ronald, Robert, Rachel

Russell, Nancy, Jo-Ann, Jeanne

This is just us, mom, dad, brothers, sisters, spouses & kids

I worked in computer operations for CVS for 18 years and then for IBM for another 18 years, till I was 'VOLUNTOLD' to retire right before Covid hit.

Not quite ready to retire, I needed to find another job.

So, I did what everyone was forced to do once Covid hit, I went online to learn to be an entrepreneur. Does this sound familiar to anyone?

Like many others I was hit by the Real Estate guru's first. I do not say that to be mean just that at the time everyone was an expert in RE and RE was booming.

I guess it wasn't for me and I was taken in a few times by the 'guru's but for the most part they knew what they were doing.

I was just not in the right mindset at the time to take advantage of it. I take full responsibility and do not consider the money spent as an expense but as an investment in my future and an expensive lesson at that.

I will show you how a newbie went from a complete novice to a $50,000 net income in just under 1 year in affiliate marketing.

That may not be everyone's dream but planting seeds along the way is a big part of getting ahead.

If you remember the movie Field of Dreams "If you build it, they will come" it works on that premise. Plant the seeds first, then nurture it and let it grow with your guidance.

It will be helpful if you have some suggestions on different products or services that you could be an affiliate for. I can do that.

Also, it will be helpful if you had some ways to meet people and join or form a tribe. I will help with that.

Getting started in something is not usually easy. I can tell you though, if you approach it with the right attitude and mindset you are so far ahead of the game. With some hints and suggestions from books like these I can just about guarantee you a good start.

AFFILIATE MARKETER ON FIRE!

It's Not About
SELLING

It's All About
TELLING

Foreword

You may remember me from being featured on the hit ABC TV show, "Secret Millionaire." If you do not know of the show, here is the basic premise from show promotions: "What happens when business motivational speaker and self-made millionaire James Malinchak is picked up by an ABC television crew, placed on an airplane with no money, credit cards, cell phone, laptop or watch, and is whisked off to an impoverished neighborhood, where he had to survive on $44.66 cents for a week?

The show features Malinchak leaving his current lifestyle in search of real-life heroes who are making a difference in their local community.

He ultimately reveals himself as a millionaire and rewards them with a portion of his own money to further their cause by gifting them with checks of his own money totaling over $100,000.

If you watched ABC's 'Secret Millionaire' you know that James is no ordinary entrepreneur. He is a self-made millionaire with a strong passion for giving back and serving others."

Amazingly, over 50 MIILLION+ people watched the show! Whether I am speaking at a conference, walking through an airport, consulting for an entrepreneur or just hanging out at a coffee shop, I always seem to get asked the same question. "What was it like being on Secret Millionaire when you had to live undercover in an impoverished neighborhood and how did it affect you?"

My answer is always the same.

The greatest gift you can have is when you simply give in order to help and serve others. There is no better feeling than when you know you have made a positive difference in lives of others.

In this book you will be inspired by JoAnn's genuine, caring nature for making a difference in your life. And her strategies can help you to achieve more than ever before.

Some strategies may comfort you while others may challenge your old paradigm. One thing is for certain. JoAnn and her strategies will stamp your spirit with an abundance of love, hope and encouragement so you can reach new levels of courage, fulfillment and personal happiness.

It is my sincere honor to introduce to you JoAnn and her brilliant book!

-James Malinchak
Featured on ABCs Hit TV Show, "Secret Millionaire" (Viewed by 50 Million+ Worldwide) Authored 25 Books, Delivered 3,000 Presentations & 2,000 Consultations Best-Selling Author, Millionaire Success Secrets Founder,
www.BigMoneySpeaker.com

Everyone is an Affiliate

Some people might argue with that statement.

But let us explore it

Do you remember Jeff Foxworthy & Bill Engvall?

"You might be a redneck if…

….and

Here's Your Sign"

Throughout this book we will play

"You might be an Affiliate If…

….so

Where's your commission?

" *You might be an Affiliate If…*

*…you read a **new book**. How long does it take you to share the book title with someone?*

Where's your commission?"

MINDSET

Most self-development books start with Mindset.

It is the most important part of getting ahead.

Recently, I saw the word ATTITUDE turned into an acronym and I had to include it here.

Cindy McLane, an accomplished and widely experienced transcriptionist, who owns a successful transcription business, says ATTITUDE stands for

"**A**ny **T**hought **T**hat **I** Th**i**nk **U**ltimat**e**ly **D**etermin**e**s **E**verything

I haven't known Cindy for long. I met her through her brother, James Malinchak, (from ABC Secret Millionaire)" but she is someone that I just clicked with right away. Sometimes it's just a good fit.

*If this piqued your interest or you know anyone who you'd like to bless by telling them about **a fast, easy painless way** to get their books transcribed - go to:*
https://affiliatemarketeronfire.com/cindymc

You must have an open mind. If your mind is already set on how affiliate marketing is NOT going to work for you, then WHY ARE YOU READING this book?

Even if affiliate marketing is the last place, you ever expected to make money, by reading this book with the right mindset, you will now be open to possibilities in your future.
Possibilities that you never would have thought of before while staying in your own niche. You can make affiliate commissions.
If I were looking back on my entrepreneur career so far, and I had to give you one piece of advice that turned my whole career around, what would it be?
I don't even have to think about it.

It would be from Jack Canfield's Book. In "The Success Principles". He has a formula he uses.

$$E + R = O \quad Event + Response = Outcome$$

The formula is referring to the fact that "You are 100% Responsible for Your Life". If you don't like your Outcome CHANGE YOUR RESPONSE

A few of you might say "Who's Jack Canfield?".

To that I would say the author of "The Chicken Soup for the Soul book series that sold over 500 million copies."
That should bring an "Oh, I know that series."
But Jack is so much more than just the author to the hugely successful and profitable series.

You can get Jack's books at:
https://bridgingthedigitalgap.com/jackc

In Jack's 'The Principles of Success Workbook' he quotes Hal Elrod:

" The moment I take responsibility for everything in my life is the moment I gain power to change anything in my life."

That is so powerful, and now you might be also asking, who is Hal Elrod? Hal wrote the "Miracle Morning Series".

He is a guest speaker I saw recently, and he was awesome. I read his first book in the series, and I am looking forward to many more from that series

If you don't want to wait you can read more about Hal's "Miracle Morning" series at
https://bridgingthedigitalgap.com/hale

Do Real Estate agents give discounts for referrals?

your dentist, doctor, hair stylist, masseuse, dance teacher, mentors?

A discount is in fact a commission. It is usually one of the very first ways people get compensated.

Most people do not even know they were acting as affiliates.

Many call them referrals instead.

I will give you some actual products and services that can make you money with a little effort on your part.

*"You might be an Affiliate If…
…you found an old-time barbershop, and you let every senior you know, know about it.
Where's your commission?"*

DEFINITION OF 'AFFILIATE MARKETER'
My Definition

My definition is sharing some good information and paying it forward so that others can receive the same benefits.

It is letting someone else 'in the loop' on something that you love or has made you incredibly happy.

This is a different view than most.

Most people when they hear the word affiliate, they **think "Oh no, another sales pitch!"**, me included, till about 2 years ago.

But I have done a complete re-adjustment.

Now, when I know someone is an affiliate, I immediately want to know what the best feature is.

With this new understanding, when I see a new product, I am interested in on the market, I reach out to see if any of my friends or acquaintances are affiliates for that product.

"You might be an Affiliate If…

…you see a Sale at your local department store and pick up the phone and tell friends and family.

Where's your commission?"

They can give me the '411' on if it is a useful product and maybe they can make a little commission as an affiliate.

If I know, like, and trust this person, then the recommendation is appreciated and welcomed.

Knowing I can earn them a commission is just a Win/Win situation.

When everyone wins, that's doing it God's Way.

You give a link for a product or service, usually on your website, but it can be in a post or comment on your social Network.

Could it be simpler? Here is a simple analogy for you.

STEP BY STEP

1. A user or customer clicks the affiliate link that is unique to you.
2. The customer makes a purchase from this link.
3. The transaction gets recorded.
4. The purchaser confirms it.
5. You get paid a pre-agreed upon commission amount.

What Is Affiliate Marketing

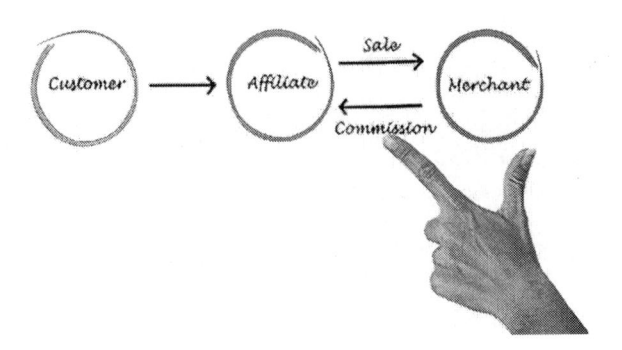

Customer → Affiliate — Sale → Merchant — Commission →

Internet Definition
What's your definition of an affiliate partner?

The Internet says:

(And the Internet is always right, right? right...;)

The affiliate partner is rewarded a payout for providing a specific result to the retailer or advertiser.

Most times, the result is a sale. But some programs can reward you for –

- Leads
- free-trial users
- clicks to a website
- getting downloads for an app.

Most affiliate programs are free to join, which takes away the worry about high startup costs.

Now in the real affiliate world out there, just because you act like an affiliate does not mean you will get monetary compensation. (In layman's terms PAID).

At least not without you taking the first step.

Normally, when someone takes you up on your suggestion, instead of a commission you would automatically feel pleasure.

- First, they value your advice.
- Second, if it's a course or group you now have an accountability partner to go with.
- Third, if you saved them the hassle of research they will be in your debt.
- Fourth, it just feels darn good to help someone.

That brings us to my next question.

If we are all naturally affiliates, in addition to the natural compensation, if they offer it, why not get a monetary one as well?

In a bit, I will tell you how that is done.

So now we have determined that we are affiliates. **What are you an affiliate for?**

If you stop and think of things that you love and would love to share with others, you will have a starting point.

(You didn't think you were going to sit here and just read, did you?)

Here are a few suggestions to start the brain waves flowing:

-Self Development Courses you took recently

-Clothing you bought

-Local gym you recently joined

-Books you recently read

-Sporting equipment you rave about

-Software you recently used

-Hairdresser you love

-Dance studio your kids go to

-Children's games that are educational

-Baby devices that saved your life

-Photographer that does the best Christmas Cards

-Horseback riding arenas

-Dog trainers

-Mentors, Coaches, Teachers

-Furniture

- Anything on AMAZON………...

-Funny things your kids say

-Special Scriptures you love

-Jewelry you want to create

Use this next page to jot down things you absolutely love that you could possibly get compensated for.

THINGS I LOVE ENOUGH TO TELL ABOUT

(Don't Sell ---- Tell)

_____

_____

_____

_____

_____

_____

_____

_____

_____

_____

_____

_____

_____

_____

_____

_____

_____

_____

ACTION!

Once your mind is set, the next most important part of getting ahead is TAKING ACTION.

Just learning something doesn't help you.

Did you take the time to fill in the blanks on the last page?

I'm just saying……… You must start somewhere.

Do this exercise, you will be that much further ahead.

It's ok, go back. I'll wait.

"You might be an Affiliate If...

…you planted flowers, and everyone wants to know where your bought them, so of course you tell them.

Where's your commission?"

BUT WAIT THERE's MORE!!!!!

I heard James Malinchak say that same thing in a webinar recently, and I said to myself "someday I am going to steal that, borrow that, model that, yeah that's it, model that" anyway I am going to use it".

There is another way to make money with affiliate marketing from the other side of the coin.

There are plenty of ways of making money, but this is just one more way.

If you have a really great product or service and your friends love it, you can set up your product or service so that you give an affiliate commission to anyone willing to promote your product.

You can now have an army of people helping you in your business and no one is being 'SALESY".

It's called earned advertising. You earned their trust. They **Tell** people about you.

They are just telling people about a product or service they love, and in the process, earn a little commission.

Life on Fire Abundance

Do we look like we might want to promote this event? (I'm in there)

As a matter of fact, this group has a 4-day Abundance convention every year in July, and I will be the first one signed up.

If you might want to hook up with a Faith Based Entrepreneur group, I would highly recommend them

https://affiliatemarketeronfire.com/lofabundance

Just knowing how something works does not mean it will work for you. So, step 1 was buying the book.

Congratulations, you're on your way to understanding affiliate marketing. Taking the next action steps means you may be on your way to becoming **A PAID AFFILIATE MARKETER!**

Affiliate Deals - Who makes out?

It is time to break down an affiliate arrangement.

We can start with the oldest arrangement in the book that everyone can identify with. Selling a HOUSE

Who are the players?

Seller　　　　Buyer　　　　Broker

SELLER - Jo-Ann & Win want the property sold (they don't want to do it themselves) & preferably with a profit = WIN

Willing to essentially 'hire' someone (RE broker) to help promote and sell the house. Although I had never thought of it this way, the RE brokers are basically the affiliates for this deal. If they don't sell the house, they don't get any money.

RE BROKERS or AFFILIATES - Chuck & Pat will get the commission for doing the work to find the buyer = WIN

As affiliates Chuck & Pat (RE Brokers) promoted to find the buyer and answer the buyers' questions.

BUYER - Peggy wants to buy a house = WIN

The affiliate or RE brokers did not have a product, yet they made a nice commission.

The buyer ended up with the house she wanted.

The seller ended up with a nice profit and gave the promised percentage in the form of a commission to the affiliate.

WIN - WIN - WIN -   God works in mysterious ways.

We were the owners and our Real Estate Agents, Chuck & Pat Vosburgh were here in Tampa, Fl this past year.
It is important, when you are learning something, to know how pertinent it is and how recent.

Especially if you were talking about online.

Things change so fast.

So as a good Affiliate marketer, I know the importance of congratulating people when it is called for.

I would like to congratulate both Chuck & Pat for recently receiving the **2021 Excellence Award in RE**.

If you are ever thinking of purchasing land in Florida, I will put the link here to make it easier for you.
https://affiliatemarketeronfire.com/vosburgh

I can totally understand how they won that award.

I forgot I was in the middle of listing a home until a week before we signed the papers. It was flawless.

I started with a Real Estate example because everyone can visualize the process.

This example is much higher on the affiliate pay scale and is not the normal, but it is the one everyone has heard of and can identify with.

You Do NOT NEED A PRODUCT to be an Affiliate.

Being a RE BROKER takes a lot of training, but normally in most affiliate deals training is minimal, so let's explore the many options where you could get started right away without training.

What does this mean to you?

There is a huge movement going on right now and it involves "bird dogs".

Do you own a home that someday you may want to sell?

Or do you know of any homes for sale where you could refer customers to a RE Agent or an investor?

A 'bird dog' is someone who could get an affiliate commission by matching RE Agents and Brokers or investors with perspective customers.

If you were a postal worker or a paper carrier, just think of all the possibilities.

How many homes on your route do you think you see that are for sale or abandoned?

Just think of the leads.

I started learning from the RE gurus, but I didn't have the right mindset then.

There are so many possibilities, that I can see myself writing another book on affiliate marketing for the RE market one day.

But one book at a time is where I will keep my focus so that I don't get overwhelmed. But I do keep a 'virtual list' for my someday ideas.

PASSIVE INCOME
Earn while you sleep?

Have you heard of "PASSIVE INCOME"? If you are like me, you had a general idea but did not really know how it worked. In a 'nutshell' PASSIVE INCOME is income **you earn** once but **get paid** on a **recurring basis**.

You always hear gurus saying, "Earn while you sleep".

What do they mean?

Sounds great right!

What are they NOT saying? Can it be that easy?

Buy it, and then go take a nap and when you wake up, you can be rich. Hmmmm…. (I do not think so… what do they know that I don't?).

Let us use me as an example of passive income (some of which I really did earn while sleeping within the last 16 months.) But I did have to plant some seeds first.

I am an affiliate for several products and services at this time, but I started as a Groove Affiliate.

I love Groove so much that I purchased a second package just for my grandkids to share and learn on.

Anyone who would like to try Groove FREE for an entire year (at the time of this printing) can check out my link at **https://affiliatemarketeronfire.com/freegroove**

Kaitlyn, Colby, Maverick, Reagan

I know in the future they will need webpages, landing pages, opt-in pages and Groove at the time of this printing, is still a LIFETIME OFFER so they are set for life.

So, Kaitlyn, Colby, Reagan, and Maverick will have access to this for an exceptionally long time. Talk about a great Investment. The future of our grandchildren.

In my wildest dreams, I did not think I would be the one to introduce them to it in my first few months with Groove.

Colby was a 10-year-old entrepreneur. He had had a few ventures so far in other areas. He gave almost all his profit to different charities.

I had to convince him that although his heart was in the right place, he needed to learn how to manage money so that it would grow for him to be able to give even more to Charity eventually.

Here is one of his rock art pieces made for me. I used to live in RI now I am in FL and I nw have my very own snowman.

When creating the Groove site, I introduced Colby to Canva which is free and a useful product. (this was pre Clickdesigns) I now upgraded for more options.

I say introduced because he took off and learned so much on his own.

If you want your FREE Canva account, check it out. Go to: https://affiliatemarketeronfire.com/canva

Colby and I did the Groove website together (we were both just beginners). We had a blast working together. When your grandchild lives 1300 miles away and you can still have this relationship you know God is watching.

This is the first page of his Groove website. Colby did all the artwork and videos himself.

If you want to take a peek at what an entrepreneur can do regardless of age, go to Colby's site: **https://affiliatemarketeronfire.com/colby**

In late 2020, I started using a product called Groove (a software package) and loved it so much I started telling others about it.

Notice I said I started 'TELLING others' about it, NOT I started 'SELLING others.' 'Selling others' is the biggest mistake I see in Affiliate marketing today.

It goes back to my original impression of an Affiliate Marketer as being 'salesy'.

Key Takeaways:

You can be an entrepreneur at any age

- You can have the heart of a child and give to Charity
- Do not keep your knowledge to yourself
- Do not believe you can't mix business with pleasure. (if it's not pleasurable why do the business?)
- Anything can be learned. "Techy" or not.
- Other tools will complement a tool you are already use

- **TELL DON'T SELL**

There is no reason to ever sell anyone on a product.

If you do sell them, then they will presume that you are responsible for their experience, and you cannot predict their experience with a product.

I know that if they buy it and it sits on a shelf, they will not make money.

I know that if they take action and learn the product or know someone who does know the product well, they can make a go of it. But not if they quit.

"You might be an Affiliate If...
... you find a new church or school, or country club and you can't wait to see if your friends know about them?

Where's your commission?"

I always want someone to buy because they want or need the product, not 'I talked them into it'.

That would not be a Win – Win scenario, therefore it is NOT 'God's Way'.

Especially this product because I and many of my friends already have made money with it. Because we did not quit.

So, if I **do not "Sell"** the product and instead I **"Tell"** them about the product, I am taking myself out of the equation.

Most times when I tell someone how much I love a product I am willing to back it up with time.

I spend time teaching them some of the ins and outs of the product.

I love to make the introduction to the product when I can. After all, I love the product, so it is actually fun to show it off. People will see the fun you are having, and it's contagious.

Your job is to inspire others to want to enjoy life.

If that means with a product you have then you have another 'Win – Win' situation.

This book will not make you a million dollars.

This book will give you a foundation.

It will show you how to 'plant the seeds' and create momentum on your way to your million dollars

You must put in the work. If you, do it right, it can be fun too.

However, you will still give your clients individual attention in other ways.

Again, that is a future book. Let us get the foundation in place first.

Just know there will come a time when you can move on to scaling where you will not need to put in actual 1 on 1 time with each client.

just start. it'll happen.

But I am assuming you are all in the initial stages and it's vital that you get the foundation planted with seeds.

Affiliate Questions? - What does an Affiliate do?

Being an affiliate means you have attached yourself to a company or person who has a product or service that:

- You like/love (or know many who do)
- You would like to help this company or person get the word out
- You tell everyone you know

If you are a PAID Affiliate you

- You would sign into the company link and get your unique affiliate link.
- You would get a commission (compensation) for giving that link away if there is a sale resulting.
- You would tell everyone in your social media what you do at some point (notice I did NOT say SELL)
- You might do demos of the product
- You might tell stories of your mentors
- You might take out ads on social media
- You cannot afford a product, but you offer to be a sub-affiliate to someone who already is an affiliate.
- You may do a YouTube video, or TikTok, or REEL etc...
- You sign up to an Online Marketplaces like Groove Marketplace, *Clickbanks, Mastermind or Amazon.*
- You might write a BOOK.

"You might be an Affiliate if...
...you have a favorite coffee shop every morning, someone new in town and you tell them about it.
Where's your commission?"

How Do You Become an Affiliate?

When I joined Groove, they had an automatic system in place that made you an affiliate. Most companies you need to apply.

I won't get paid unless I take action, which in this case meant going to find my affiliate link on their site and putting it somewhere where it could be found. Which I did.

For most companies, you would search on the website for 'affiliate' and they will have specific instructions on how you can sign up.

Most times it is FREE to be an affiliate.

I received this post from one of the partners in Groove before I even hit 5 figures.

(You have been an inspiration to watch grow... you get "Most Improved Groovester" for March)

Joe Jalonski
You have been an inspiration to watch grow...you get "Most Improved Groovester" for March

Joe Jalonski
You have been an inspiration to watch grow...you get "Most Improved Groovester" for March

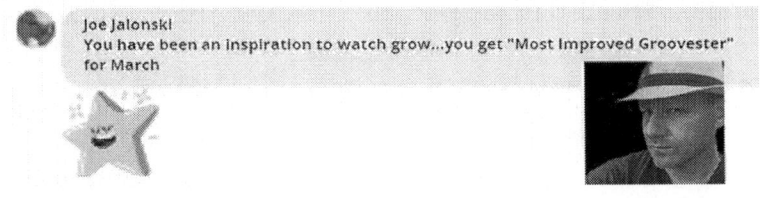

Joe Jablonski was the Director of Affiliates when I started and when you can work with someone inside the company whose agenda is the same as yours, that's what you are looking for.

Thank you, Joe, for your support.

Joe was a big part of my success with Groove.

Joe has made some of the props I use in my videos check him out at https://affiliatemarketeronfire.com/joej

How Much Money Can I Make?

Every product or service is unique. I can only tell you that I made over $50,000 in my 1st year as an affiliate.

This was my first 5 figure paycheck.

> Congratulations... Your affiliate payment is on the way!
> **Vendor:** Mike Filsaime
> **Amount:** $10157.8   **$10,157.80**
> **Payment method:** Paypal
> **Payment date:** 01 Jul 2021 02:05 pm EDT   **01 July 2021**

This is not common but many of my friends (who were once and still are my mentors) have made 10 to 20 times that amount in the same amount of time with the some of their products. (More on this later)

> Congratulations... Your affiliate payment is on the way!
> **Vendor:** Mike Filsaime
> **Amount:** $11697.6   **$ 11,697.60**
> **Payment method:** Wire
> **Payment date:** 30 Oct 2021 05:38 pm EDT   **30 Oct 2021**
> **Message:** Wise
> Thank you very much for your affiliate support!

I am in the infancy of my pursuit of affiliate marketing. Full transparency, they were late with payment so it included extra time to earn.

Who Do I Model After?

I spent a lot of time reading about the millionaires and how they spend their day.

I used to follow people like Tony Robbins. As a matter of fact, I have been following him since the 1980's when he courses came out in cassette tapes.

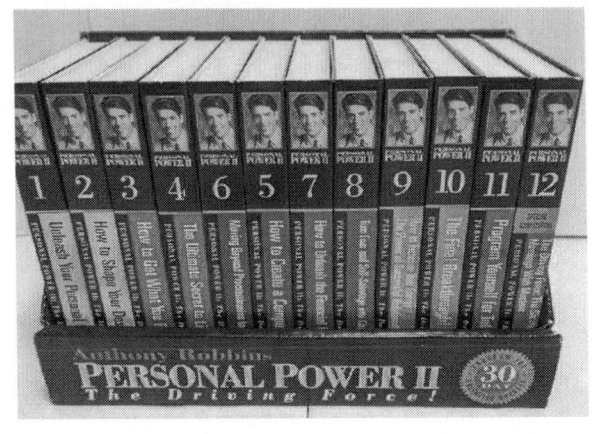

I credit him with my start & some 'Wins'. But you don't just read books. That was my mistake in the 1980's.

Reading is not going to get you anywhere.

You want to also add to those teachings a more accessible mentor that will be available to you.

Sometimes I prefer to know how, ordinary people like you and me spend our day and make it rich somehow.

People who have only recently got a good handle on it, so I can model their efforts.

Yes, modeling Millionaires is good, but they have already 'scaled'.

Most (not all) are almost impossible to talk to in person.

You jump through so many hoops and mostly end up with their membership advisors.
I get it, the ideal goal is to NOT be available to everyone and to guard your time.

At this time of my life, I found that following newer success stories, people who may have made a million dollars but so recently that they are not considered 'Set for life'.

These people are still working hard for the 'paycheck' so they can be financially set soon but **they are not there yet.**

Above you will find 3 AMAZING mentors. I have not asked but I am pretty sure they have all made over a million dollars in affiliate/online marketing. (Maybe 10x's that) And yet, look at us all on a call and them picking on me. It was a blast.

CoachDeb, Alicia Lyttle & Angie Norris will not be strangers to this book.

These coaches/mentors are 'available' to talk to you.

While you are coming up the ladder, it is crucial that you meet as many people as possible.

Below you will see a coaching class by Coach Megan (The Queen of Coaching). Look at our expressions.

Now this is the way to learn.

I took steps that lined me up with my mentors. The end results of the actions I took gave me the 'secret' of how to get ahead.

All the people mentioned in this book are great mentors and accessible to you when you become a student.

But you need to find out so much about yourself before you can decide on who would be best to model.

"You might be an Affiliate If...
...you have a new teacher/mentor in class today that was so awesome you want to tell the world?
Where's your commission?"

How do I Replicate?

I have always been interested in self-development. You can see as far back as 40 years ago, 'Anthony Robbins'.

What is different now?   I am not just listening.
**I am DOING SOMETHING about it.
I am taking ACTION.**

If I had a nickel for every instructor that told me to take action, I would be rich.

Why did I not listen to them earlier?
Wait for it.........
MINDSET (oh no, here it is again!)

The main reason my life is so good right now, is not only because I resourced up (which I understand may take you time to get there), but I resourced up slowly and every single person I took as my mentor has been accessible to me personally.
Now when I purchase a course, I jump in with both feet.

"You might be an Affiliate If...

...you see an airline having an anniversary sale which is a 'no brainer' and can't wait to tell everyone you know.

Where's your commission?"

Lessons You Should Not Follow

After jumping in - What should you NOT do?

When joining something, a course, a Facebook page, group or Zoom session:

-You should NOT be the quiet flower on the wall.

-You should NOT sit back and watch the chat go by.

-You should NOT join their Facebook page and not post.

-You should NOT worry about the others in the group if they have made more progress than you.

-You should NOT make excuses for not getting assignments done.

-Session chats are NOT the time to be selling your stuff. Networking (which should be more relationship building) is done, before or after the session NOT during the session.

-Never put your link in a Session chat for someone else's webinar.

-A huge insult to everyone in the class especially the instructor. Unless the instructor invites you to.
-Do not monopolize the conversation.
-It's important that the host remains the host in the group.

Lessons You Should Follow
After Jumping IN - What should you do?

When joining something, a course, a Facebook Page, Group, or a zoom session:

-Be aware if the Session chat is meant for networking or teaching.

-You SHOULD post and introduce yourself IMMEDIATELY in the Group page and then again in a week for those who came in the group late.

-As others introduce themselves, welcome them, encourage them, engage with them

-During the classes PAY ATTENTION to the Lesson.

-Identify yourself in the session chat as to where you are from, before the Session starts.

-The instructors love the chat being busy, but they want you to be discussing what they are teaching once class starts nothing else.

-Once you answer someone's post or they answer yours, look up their profile.

-If they are not friends, now is the best time to invite them.

-They now know, like and on their way to trusting you.

MY BEGINNINGS:

Recently, I was one of 104 contributors to a book called LIVE ABUNDANTLY.

You can a free list of all the contributors at https://affiliatemarketeronfire.com/contributors

When the book first came out someone said 'Oh that's too bad you are at the end of the book'.

I guess that was one way to look at it.

Because they went alphabetically, I was placed as the very last contributor in the book.

In her mind that was a negative but in my mind I had the advantage.

- I would be the last person they think of when they finally get the good feeling of finishing something. (the book).

- I will be fresh on their minds if they wanted to go look me up.

- If it made this person notice who was last, how many others will notice me?

When I contributed to the book I must have been in this exact state of mind.

I am going to copy a portion of my article because it tells of exactly where I was when I decided to become an entrepreneur.

"You might be an Affiliate if…

…you just sold your house using a Real Estate Agent and you tell your neighbors about them.

Where's your commission?"

Excerpt from LIVE ABUNDANTLY!

HOW WOULD YOU feel if you lost your dad, your job, and your car in the same summer?

- *I focused on the six incredible months I got to spend with my dad, who was 87 and only sick those last few days.*

- *I focused on the 41 resource actions I survived the previous 9 years with IBM (while receiving numerous awards), before finally being "VOLUNTOLD" to retire?*

- *I focused on the fact that no one was hurt. My car was old, and I was gifted a newer one to replace it.*

Where would your focus have been?

There were over 100 of us who contributed to that book. If you know one of us, go and purchase from them or you can purchase from me here: https://affiliatemarketeronfire.com/live

Everything in life depends on how you think about it.

The situation can be the same and 2 people will walk away with different feelings. We alw0ays come back to MINDSET.

What did that mean for me?

- Now my time was freed up (although I would much rather have continued spending it with dad, but he was at peace now starting his next journey).

- I no longer had a job to go to either. (Extra time on my hands).

- And no money coming in.

- Does this sound familiar to any of you?

Like so many of you, I decided to improve myself.

What does that actually mean?

Self-Development courses of course.

Let me guess.... You are too!   No surprise there.

You can't look at the Internet without getting hit from all sides.

So, I went down that 'rabbit hole'.

Hours and hours of time looking at FREE challenges that turned out to be NOT so FREE.

"You might be an Affiliate If...
...you found a bank that was actually paying a good interest rate, so you pass out that bank name for them.

Where's your commission

Which Course Should You Take?

It's not so much which courses you take as it is, what will you do after taking the course.

Online learning has come a long way and I would highly recommend before signing up for a course, that if you can take a FREE webinar or challenge with that instructor, you do.

There are just too many courses out there to take the first shiny object you see.

There are many ways to be an affiliate such as Groove Marketplace, amazon, Clickbank, JVzoo, Shareasale, or Warrior+, but those are not the direction this book will be taking today.

Although, I am signed up for a few of them, I always like to thoroughly research before I recommend to anyone. (Next book!)

I will be taking you along what I know best of Affiliate Marketing in your own neighborhood using organic contacts instead of paid advertising.

Then I will show you how I expanded my 'organic' reach from hundreds to over 3300 'social media friends' while gaining know, like and trust.

Also, how to reach hundreds of thousands of like-minded people but not in a 'salesy" way.

We will use the 'Give First Method" or as I lovingly call it "God's Way'

"You might be an Affiliate If...
...you know a startup business who could use some affiliates to get them started so you get them some.

Where's your commission?"

During my very first Free Webinar that I attended, I signed up for a paid course with Jon Talarico.

It was a smaller Founders' class (under 20 people I believe) and we all had personal attention.

Jon knew what was going on with us. He personally texted me when my niece was in the hospital checking on her progress.

Boy, was I spoiled, I thought all courses were going to be like this.

NOT!

Remember what I say about Founders' deals, they are the best.

One of Jon's teachings got me started on my Gratitude Log and today is gratitude # 7810.

Tips:

- When you attend Zooms take screenshots.
- Go out of your way to meet the others in class?
- Take advantage of all the like minded people.
- Join the dedicated Facebook page

That course was 16 months ago

This zoom picture below is only a few weeks ago.

Here are 6 of his original students who STILL meet today, weekly to touch base. (I am in the middle).

Jon taught us some great skills about relationship building.

Do you remember your first webinar?

Are you still practicing anything from it?

Are you still in touch with anyone you met that day?

That's how you know when a mentor or webinar has done its job.

Anyone can go to a webinar and listen and love it, but 2 days later will you remember any of it?

Two years later I am still practicing Jon's teachings.

Jon is known as "The Connector".

One of his projects is called "A Million in You".

If you want to be an affiliate marketer, having connector skills can be extremely useful.

Think about it, you know all the players, you can connect people in so many different fields and ways.

It's a Win – Win situation (remember God's way everyone needs to win).

I think about it occasionally and Thank God that Jon was my first experience in the scary world of Entrepreneurship.

The world of Overwhelm (if you let it).

Watching everyone else get wins before me and wondering WHY?

Wanting to celebrate with them but sometimes you can't help but wish it were you.

Does any of this sound familiar to anyone. Relax, it is totally normal. We all go through it. Just remember to do it God's Way and things fall back into place.

I didn't think about it until right now, but Jon is probably one of the reasons I ended up as an affiliate or a "Connector".

If I haven't said it before "Thank you Jon Talarico".

One of the handouts from Jon was "10 Laws of Connecting". To download a free copy or just learn more about Jon you can visit **https://affiliatemarketeronfire.com/jon**

"You might be an Affiliate If
… You watched a building being torn down and were so impressed with the destruction team that you recommend them as you tell the story of the building collapse
Where's your commission?"

Bucket List Item

Did you ever have something on your bucket list that you never really expected to come true.

My success as an entrepreneur is directly related to one of my bucket lists items.

Let me tell you about one of my items.

I have a friend named Cynda Teachman Harris from Grow Life Coaching Networking here in the Tampa FL area.

On my bucket list was to get certified as a life coach.

I have always admired Cynda and when we moved to Fl in 1997, Cynda's family was one of the very first to take our family in to their home.

Not just our son, who was best friends with their son. But they made sure we fit in. For that and so much more I will be forever grateful.

Again, why is that important to you?

Have you ever just picked up and moved to a new state thousands of miles away?

It is scary and gets lonely fast.

We were so Blessed to have found Cynda's family.

Certifying life coaches was Cynda's specialty for years and I had to watch from a distance because I had the 9-5 job for ever.

Now I had the opportunity. The weekend for Certification had arrived. It was a 50-minute drive, and I didn't want to be late, so I got there few hours early and had lunch.

During lunch I received a call that Cynda just returned from the doctor. They found a huge brain tumor.

Goes without saying, our class was called off and Cynda was in for a long haul.

Cynda's outlook did not look great, but her journey would not be alone.

After months & months & months of surgery and procedures with 2 steps forward 1 step back, with God's good Grace, not to mention the thousands of Prayer Warriors out there, Cynda made it through.

Right before Christmas, I was made a certified life coach from this incredible miracle of a human being.

If you would like more information on Cynda you can connect with this miracle of a lady at https://affiliatemarketeronfire.com/cynda

To watch her incredible journey and know she never, ever lost Faith that God was carrying her along the roughest parts was a gift to me.

I am not sure if I learned more in her actual class or by just watching how she handle this emergency.

What steps she took with her family, her friends, her business and of course her complete FAITH that God had her and she was going to be fine.

Why did I tell you this? How can this help your business?

Do you think Cynda is the only one to ever get bad news while putting on an Event?

Literally, hours away from the event and somehow through it all, she fulfilled her commitment and has our undying trust in all she does.

She could offer a course tomorrow and I wouldn't care the subject. I would purchase it. In business, people are watching you.

They watch how you teach:
- How you react to bad news
- How you fulfill your promises
- If you take the easy road or stick with your project
- How you deal with delays

Not worrying about what others think is a skill.

Some people will never conquer that skill

You need to always live your life with integrity because no matter what they see, they will have their own opinion.

If you are in integrity with yourself, the rest is between you and God.

The bible tells us to live in God's Image.

What Do You Do While Waiting?

I had caught the entrepreneur bug after Jon's class.

I still wanted to continue my education while waiting for Cynda to recover.

When you are actively pursuing something and you come up against a 'roadblock', what is your reaction?

Do you wait and lose all your momentum? Not me.

I was online and saw a 7-day Free Challenge.

How many Free Challenges have you taken that lead to an upsell and the next morning you had 'Buyer's Remorse'?

Well, this WASN'T one of them.

- Yes, it was a free challenge
- Yes, they had an upsell and
- Yes, I chose the upsell

- BUT this was not an expense to me. This was an **INVESTMENT.** I am worth it! I took out my credit card and purchased the upsell and I never looked backed!
-

Why was this considered an investment and most of the other programs an expense?

That's easy – MINDSET (my mindset)

- If you took the challenge and you did NOT engage during the challenge
- If you did NOT join the Facebook Group unique to this challenge
- If you did NOT do the nightly assignments
- If during the challenge, you were in 2 meetings at one time.
- If you took phone calls or answered texts time
- If you never took your notebook out

If you have too many yeses above, you would be wasting your money to buy the upsell.

This goes for any course you invest in out there.

Because you didn't put any effort into bettering yourself when it was free what makes you think you will now?

Again, I jumped in with both feet.

I no longer considered the money I spent an expense it was an investment in myself. I am worth it!

If you said "yes" to those questions, it would not be an investment for you.

If this is the way you attend a FREE webinar, then any course you are thinking of putting your money into should be used on something else.

It's not the challenge or the course, it's you.

Your heart isn't in it.

Your 'WHY" is not defined enough yet.

Finding your 'Why" is extremely important and is part of MINDSET". We will not be going into that in this book however, you should know your Why.

That 7-day free challenge led me to Life on Fire. Which is a faith-based entrepreneur group owned and run by Nick & Megan Unsworth. More info later in the book on these two incredible people.

Joining this group was probably one of the best moves I have ever made. I found a family of like-minded entrepreneurs who are all putting God first.

"You might be an Affiliate If...

... your friend is a coach, and you see someone desperately in need of one and you match them up.

Where's your commission?"

Finding your "Why" and then doing something about it was a huge part of the challenge.

If you would like a download with some nuggets I learned from the Free Challenges or more on Life on Fire, go https://affiliatemarketeronfire.com/lofabundance

To recap:

- When I started with Groove, they had an 'OTO' (one time offer)
- They had a Lifetime Membership for one price
- They had bells and whistles that I had never heard of

I decided I would try it for FREE.

If you want to try it free you can access it at https://affiliatemarketeronfire.com/freegroove

I saw **a FREE Summit** advertised just a few days later.

What happens at a FREE Summit?   UPSELLS!

Did I learn my lesson? NOPE

I promised myself before I sat down, that I would not buy.

How many times have you done that?

Does this sound familiar to anyone?

Guess who comes on as one of the many speakers.

Jon Talarico, my very first mentor in entrepreneurship.

But luckily his upsell was the same one I had just taken, and I was still involved.

Thinking I was off the "upsell hook", Jon introduced the next speaker who was his good friend Alicia Lyttle.

What did that do for Alicia?

- She immediately had some clout because Jon trusts her, and I trust Jon.
- So, as I was listening, she didn't have to tell me about herself, just the product.
- What do you think that product was?

GROOVE

You guessed it. She was promoting the Groove App that I was just looking into and if you have never heard Alicia speak, you are definitely missing something.

She could convince eskimos to buy ice in December.

She takes you right into the product and does demo's so there is no mystery in what you are buying.

She offered several weeks of support for the product.

In addition, she is the master of bonuses.

She added so many bonuses that I didn't care what the product was at this point I only wanted the bonuses.

Alicia Lyttle is an incredible marketer, and I had no idea that I was 'Alice falling down the rabbit hole' when I was lucky enough to meet her and her sister Lorette (who has taken marketing to a new high).

"You might be an Affiliate If…

,,,you went to a 2-day mastermind in a mansion and couldn't stop telling everyone about the program.

Where's your commission?"

Alicia and I. our 1st meeting. An introduction I will forever cherish.

They have so much knowledge on marketing, that I have been in awe of their accomplishments from the day I met them.

Currently, Alicia's taking some of her energy into the Real Estate world. (Remember the first example in this book?)

If she is this good at marketing, I am going to being keeping a very close eye on her.

Lorette and I on our 1st meeting and the start of a long and lasting friendship.

If you would like to contact the Lyttle Sisters, go to https://affiliatemarketeronfire.com/alicia

How does Alicia's story help you?

- First, she had an introduction from a trusted source. There was no need for me to doubt her integrity.
- She knew her product very well.
- She gave a demonstration of her product in a matter of minutes.
- She knew that if you are going to give a bonus to make it be so valuable that there was no doubt you were getting 2, 4 even 6 times in value above and beyond what you are paying for it.
- She made sure you had some support available once you purchased
- It is very, very **important to surround yourself with people who are where you want to be.**

So of course, out came my visa card and the Groove Lifetime Offer was bought by my business.

Has this ever happened to you?

There are so many bonuses that you forgot what you are buying? I have decided to do that as well. Offer bonuses.

Have you fallen down that "Shiny Object Syndrome" hole?

I cannot tell you how many times that happened to me and in the morning, I usually have "Buyers' Remorse".

That was a real thing for me. "Buyers' Remorse"

Until .... wait for it!
I changed my **MINDSET**.

I did it!

I drop that word that we all dread when taking a self-development course.   MINDSET.

It seems you can never get to the 'meat and potatoes' till they make sure you have the right MINDSET.

Why is that do you think?

Could they ALL have a point, or could they ALL be wrong? I finally got it and once I did, YIKES!

So, if you saw the word mindset and you said, "YES I need to keep reading because Mindset is ALWAYS the first step to EVERYTHING IN LIFE". Kudo's.

Then my friend congratulations you are already on the right track, and I will give you as many golden nuggets as you are willing to pick up.

But if you saw the word MINDSET and said,

"OH No, not again, please just skip that and give me the affiliate tips I asked for" then you have some work to do.

Because even if I give you all the greatest tips in the world in this book, if your mindset is not in the right place these tips won't work.

"You might be an Affiliate if...

...while giving a webinar, you mention a book you loved and recommended it.
Where's your commission?"

I have to laugh now because at least the first 5 or 6 courses I took I had that "**Oh No, attitude**" when I came to the Mindset.

BUT there is hope, I promise.

- Mindset is totally up to you, so you decide now.

- Will you keep an open mind and not talk yourself out of every good idea that comes up?

- Will you have a positive thought instead of **"I've already tried that, and it didn't work"**.

- Try saying **"I tried something like that, if I evaluate it again and see what I could have done differently, things would have come out differently."**

- Take the *t* out of can't. It really can make all the difference in the world.

    I am just saying DO NOT COUNT YOURSELF OUT.

"You might be an Affiliate If...
...you are travelling with a friend and constantly introduce him as a 'bestselling author' to everyone you meet.

Where's your commission?"

Your mind can be your friend or your enemy, **you get to decide.**

It must be true I read it online

Why would you......?

That's a scam......

My buddy did that once....

I remember doing that...

Most times we listen to our friends and family and other naysayers telling how something will never work.

Here's how to judge if you should listen to them.

- Are they financially where you want to be?

- Are they spiritually where you want to be?

- Are they heading in the right direction?

- If not, why are you wasting your time listening to them. Yes, I understand you can still be their friend, but you don't need to take their advice unless they are where you want to be.

"You might be an Affiliate
...you found a dry cleaner that delivers at no charge, so you recommend them

Where's your commission?"

How Did I find a Product to Sell?

How did I go from no income to $50,000 in under one year, when I didn't even truly know what an affiliate marketer was, and I didn't have a product of my own?

Let me educate you a little on what OTO and Lifetime offers mean.

OTO - One Time Offers are usually the best you will see for a particular product and when possible, you should think twice about turning it down.

If they happen to include in that One Time Offer a Lifetime Offer, it's usually as I like to call 'a no-brainer'

OTO usually means:

- They will only offer this particular deal 1X
- They always put a deadline for urgency's sake
- It's usually a very good deal
- Almost always, they will attach Bonuses if you buy now
- I usually watch the new classes and courses to see if they are using OTO on everything they do. I like to deal with companies with integrity.
- It's important if you say it's an OTO that you honor it.

LIFETIME OFFER means:

- If you buy this product, you will always have this access if the product is on the market or is in existence (what's called the life of the product.)
- So, you pay once and never pay for this again.
- Some products will include all updates to that product
- Lifetime offers are usually attached to the launch of a product. They want to fill their funnel faster, so the best deals always come when a company is just starting up.

Once I joined the Academy program, I knew it was only a matter of time till I needed a website and had no clue how to do that.

Are any of you in that position right now. How the heck do I create a website? What platform or app do I use?

Part of the membership was 14 days free to try out the recommended software.

Then it would be $99 or $299 a month and I was nervous about the monthly expense.

This is the main reason I even tried Groove.

As it was, I put the Academy cost on my credit card in monthly payments.

Have you ever wanted something so badly that you know you shouldn't, but you use a credit card to get it?

That was the same week the ad for GrooveFunnels came across my desk, The rest is history. Groove was the lesser of my financial debate.

Meet Groovezilla (Groove's mascot)

Along the way I started following Angie Norris.

Angie is the First Ambassador for Groove (among other things) and I have seen her all over the place.

I learned things from watching her and visiting her groups that have made huge differences in my career.

Even if they are the smallest tweaks.

As my mentor Nick says "sometimes it just needs a little tweaking"

Angie showed me the importance of taking advantage of every piece of what she calls 'Real Estate' you have.

In this case she was talking about your Facebook Cover.

We all have one, but are we all utilizing it correctly?

When you are an affiliate marketer this is the perfect place to showcase one of your products or services.

You could change this cover every few weeks, so people don't get used to it and ignore it.

You could make it engaging.

I took Angie's advice and I decided to showcase my Groove affiliate link and my successes at the same time.

I shortened my affiliate link. Most affiliate links are long and let's face it ugly.

What do you do with your shorten link once you have it?

I started to change my Facebook cover so people could know what I do and see my progress as well.

"You might be an Affiliate If...

... you took a yoga or karate class this week and asked a friend to come with you because it has helped you so much.

Where's your commission?"

This turned out to be genius.

Because, they were now able to take a journey with

> Congratulations! You've made a sale as an affiliate!
> Product
> Sale Amount: $1397.00
> Your commission: $558.40
>
> 4 X's and counting
>
> This Happened Nov 4, Nov 7, Nov 11 & Nov 23, 2020a

I showed my first affiliate commission check and then mentioned that I did this 4 times so far and I put the dates.

This now replaced my Facebook Cover, and I added my shortened affiliate link https://bit.ly/freefrommejw *in my bio right there on the cover.*

If you would like Free instructions on how to shorten your links go to ***https://affiliatemarketeronfire.com/shorten***

Each month after I made sales, I intended to update it.

"You might be an Affiliate If…
…. you took an Uber last night and get your drivers name to share.
Where's your commission?"

Let's RECAP:

- Your Facebook Page has valuable Real Estate, and you need to take advantage of it. (Why not put this book down and go take action, at least jot down in your journal to do this later).

- Take your followers on a journey with your Facebook cover

- Naysayers are a part of life

- You get to decide who you want to listen to

- Change your Facebook cover picture either monthly or every few months

- Mix up your posts on your Facebook page, some personal, some business, some quotes

- The idea is to get others to engage with you.

- Put up 2 of an object and ask for an opinion on which is better. Everyone loves to give their opinion (just remember you really don't need their opinion because you may already know which one you like)

- Not everything you read online has to be true.

If you have never created a Facebook cover and want FREE help, go to:
https://affiliatemarketeronfire.com/fbcover

GETTING YOUR FIRST SALES

On promotion day while I was in our (LOF) Faith Based Group, I saw a beautiful cross come across my screen.

I loved it so much that I took the link and posted on my Facebook page and said that "I hope my husband sees this because my birthday was coming up."

Like a good husband, he took the hint and purchased $60.00 worth of beautiful jewelry for my birthday.

Well, a few days later I receive a commission ticket from Groove

Congratulatios! You've made a sale as an affiliate!

Congratulations! You've made a sale as an affiliate!

Product : GrooveFunnels Lifetime Upgrade

Sale Amount : $1397.00   **$ 1,397.00**

Your commission : $558.80   **$ 558.00**

I was blown away. I had no clue where this came from.

Angel Baratta (the jewelry owner) was in the same faith based entrepreneur group I was in

- She was starting up a new company
- We were her first sale on this new adventure in life.
- She had a new business and needed a website
-

She wanted to know who purchased from her and went to my webpage.

Angel has a Facebook page for **Rejuvenate and Revitalize your Life with Angel**

Remember one of the first things I learned from Angie Norris was to have a link on your Facebook cover.

To be a good affiliate normally:

- You sign up for a product or service

- You go sign in and find the affiliate link

- You make the link a 'short link' (no one likes long ugly links) and put on your Social Media profiles.

- You start giving that link out to anyone who may benefit (Notice I didn't say just everyone, don't lead with a salesy attitude.) Who do you know that you could benefit?

My Facebook cover was advertising for free Groove web sites, and she needed a website for her new business.

We spent $60 and made $558 in commissions that day. (Literally, I made money that night in my sleep).

If you have been paying attention so far, you would have picked up on the fact that a good affiliate marketer always helps their listener get easy access to whatever great product or person is involved.

This serves several purposes.

First, it introduces you to some great people and products.

If you did your homework for helping these people get ahead, they probably will give you a commission (especially if you are set up as their affiliate).

So now let's recap.

- You find someone or something that is awesome.
- You tell 1, 2 and 3 people about them or the product.
- They someday down the road purchase what they have.
- You get a commission because they used your unique link.
- The special someone or the product gets a new client or customer.
- They get access to a great mentor or product.
  WIN - WIN - WIN   all the way around.

So, if that is the way it is done, and I loved this jewelry so much why haven't I told you the name of the jewelry company?

GLAD YOU ASKED.

Right about now my process would be to reach out to the service or product holder and ask how they would like to be reached. Then add them to the book.

I reached out to Angel and in addition to giving me the website for the jewelry she mentioned "if you know anyone who would like to buy me out, I would be in the market," I now have a new niche.

I immediately decided to help her out and buy her out.

Little did I know what possibilities would be opening from this.

You start to see opportunities in everything.

What did I see here (after the fact of course)?

- I now have jewelry inventory to give as bonuses.
- I have jewelry inventory to sell online as a business.
- I have jewelry inventory to give as Christmas or birthday presents.
- I received all her marketing materials.
- I have jewelry inventory to give away as prizes.
- I have jewelry to wear, we already established that I love the jewelry.

All of this is happening because I was reaching out to her to help give her some exposure in my book.

I wanted to thank her for being my 1st affiliate for Groove.

But I ended up offering to help her by buying her out so she can attend to her new ventures.

All Win – Win but who really Won?

I did!

I was helping out a friend and I ended up with so many opportunities

There is a reason this book is subtitled

"Using the Give First Model (God's Way)"

No matter what I do, it always comes back and blesses me.

Writing this book is so much fun. I love sharing the good, other people do.

This book is a perfect opportunity to help you learn by using real examples. Win – Win – Win God's Way.

How Long Does It Take for a 2nd Sale?

A few weeks after I purchased Groove, is when I met Angel and her jewelry.

Less than 7 days later I was talking with another member in one of the many groups I now belong to.

Michael Witt wondered if we could start a group of like-minded people and was asking for someone's input.

I jumped in and we started a Facebook group.

Once I started posting in the group, he and I started talking about Groove and within no time at all he purchased.

I now had my second commission check in less than a week.

> **Congratulatios! You've made a sale as an affiliate!**
>
> Congratulations! You've made a sale as an affiliate!
>
> Product : GrooveFunnels Lifetime Upgrade
>
> Sale Amount : $1397.00   **$ 1,397.00**
>
> Your commission : $558.80   **$ 558.00**

I didn't spend a cent, all I had to do was let Michael know what I do, and he was in the market for a website anyway and wanted to give me the commission.

Get used to telling people what you do, but please remember to invest time in them first. Get to know them and what they do.

Relationship building is more than 95% of affiliate marketing.

By creating this group with Michael, we were able to fill in each other's blind spots.

Meaning we combined our knowledge of our own unique experiences.

This was the beginning of our first 'tribe'.

"You might be an Affiliate If...
...you had your family photo done. It came out great. You show them all around with the photographer's card.

Where's your commission?"

Third times a CHARM: This happened while attending a webinar for another entrepreneur named Stephen M. Law.

After the webinar, we hit it off and found out he lives within 15 minutes of my home.

That weekend he was doing a book signing on his very first book and invited me to come.

It was almost the exact same scenario as Angel. I loved the book signing environment and bought 4 books.

My son Core is also a local Pastor, so I bought a book for a few church members.

Again, I was the first one there and his first sale.

Without telling me Stephen looked me up in Facebook and saw my link.

Of course, Stephen was a new entrepreneur and could use a website app. . (now he has **http://www.outdo.life**) look him up.

Guess what showed up in my email a few days later?

> Congratulations! You've made a sale as an affiliate!
>
> Product ████████████
>
> Sale Amount : $1397.00
>
> Your commission : $558.80

Ok so you get the picture. If you were following along you will see that I spend $1397.
And in 3 weeks of commissions, I earned $1,676.40

Giving me a profit of $279.40 plus unlimited Groove websites for life.   **"MIKE DROP"**

Did I mention that I really couldn't afford the $1,397 so I put it on a credit card.?

Why do think I told you about all 3 of my first sales?

There must be a lesson here right.

"You might be an Affiliate If…

…you attended a wedding and really like the DJ. Who you gonna tell?

Where's your commission?"

To recap what happened:

- You need **to join a group** of likeminded people.
- You need to **respond to requests in post**.
- Or from Angel's point you need **to post when you have something others would like**. (Without spamming or selling).
- You need to reach out when you see something to **make a connection with someone**. I stumbled across that jewelry because Angel had a picture of it online.
- You need to have **your social media ready** should anyone stumble on your page. She stumbled onto my Groove link because I had it strategically placed on my Social Media account.
- You need to **attend other people's webinars** and contact as many people as you can. I found out Stephen had a book signing that weekend because I attended a webinar. We discovered we lived in the same area.
- You need to **have your affiliate links available** and in plain sight. You should make nice short links and have them on all your profiles.
- You need to **answer other people's questions** in their posts and when you can offer to serve them with what they need. Michael wanted a partner to run a Facebook group and even if I had never done that before I offered.

"You might be an Affiliate If…

…. you go to a new dentist and didn't feel a thing during the whole visit? I'll bet next time you hear someone needs a dentist you will have his/her name on your lips.

Where's your commission?"

To recap what DIDN'T happened:

- You don't need your own product.
- You don't need to advertise and spend big bucks
- You don't need to have a huge email list to start (I didn't know anyone of these 3 people)
- You don't need to plaster your face all over social media
- You don't need to charge someone just because you are helping them out.
- You don't need to parade your kids online by using them like pawns. Celebrate them online.
- You don't need to buy expensive software when you just start out (maybe never, depends on your direction)
- You don't need a large staff
- You don't need a VA (Virtual Assistant) until you are so busy it would free up your time for more money producing activities

KEEP IT SIMPLE

"You might be an Affiliate If......

... you had your yard professionally landscaped, and everyone wants the name of your landscaper.

Where's your commission?"

Off to the Races RIGHT!

WRONG!

I guess by now I am looking like I have a great mindset and I am flying high.

Just because I got lucky and made 3 or 4 commission checks did not make me a good affiliate marketer.

It made me a lucky one.

All those lessons I just documented were mostly done by accident. I learned them while I was doing them or after the fact, I figured out why they worked.

Granted, I did need to do some work, so it wasn't all luck. For instance,

- I knew enough to go find my affiliate link.
- I knew enough to shorten my affiliate link.
- I knew enough to talk to people about what I do.
- I knew enough to get my shortened affiliate link out where people could find it.

But that really was the extent of my affiliate training. I was a newbie let's face it.

I had some success. I got all my money back for the product. I wasn't thinking of myself as an affiliate marketer. I was still finding my niche.

Was it coaching, courses, books? I was still clueless.

You might be an Affiliate if...

---you saw a band at a nightclub and suggests them to a buddy who needs one.

Where's your commission?"

WHAT TO DO NEXT

Since I had no clue what a goldmine Groove was, I took Groove and put it up on the 'virtual shelf'.

I continued my training to be a coach and joined every single new shiny object out there.

I learned about how to use Groove.

I had started following Angie Norris, and Alicia Lyttle closer.

You've seen this picture earlier.

What you didn't know about it is that I didn't do LIVE's at the time.

This was the first time I was on Live with them.

I was adamant and never going to talk online or in a video. That was not going to happen.

They 'forced me,' kiddingly of course, to join them on that zoom call which was being broadcast live on Facebook to all 3 of their tribes.

My Life on Fire mentor, Nick Unsworth was constantly telling us that going online to introduce ourselves to the group would go a long way in expanding our email lists and our contacts.

But I wasn't having any of it.

No Nick, I don't do lives". That became my mantra."

Does it sound like someone needed a **MINDSET** change? YUP, big time.

A new Platform was in Town

Clubhouse was new back then and there was a 3 -6 month waiting list to get invited into Clubhouse. (It was like a private club, a zoom call without the video).

These three, who I lovingly call my 3 Heroes, figured out a way to make a Clubhouse train and got dozens and dozens of people in one zoom session into Clubhouse.

Join the next trains http://clubhousetrain.com

They saw a platform being born and the millions of opportunities that brought.

Why is any of this important to an affiliate marketer?

They collaborated. Three power ouses. You already met Alicia Lyttle and Angie Norris and later in the book you will meet (CoachDeb) Deb Cole.

In my opinion, my 3 heroes are 3 of the best affiliate marketers to model out there.
- They learned the Platform.
- They wrote the very first book on Clubhouse together.
- They created a Facebook group.
- They created a blog for clubhouse.
- Everything they did was by way of meeting new people and serving these people while never asking for a penny.
- They create a tribe that now follows all 3 of them, by combining their resources.
- The waiting list of Clubhouse was 6 months long. Yet they figured a way to get hundreds of their tribe in, in just a few weeks.

But that doesn't tell you how I ended up on that Zoom/Facebook live call.

I was the 1st passenger they let on the train. Mostly because I was Alicia's affiliate, and I was very persistent.

I had been waiting for weeks to get an invite to Clubhouse.

Once in Clubhouse, there were so many things to learn. I was short on time and wanted as many shortcuts as I could get.

Does this sound familiar to you? TIME is PRECIOUS
You might be an Affiliate If…

…you get a new dress and matching shoes for the prom, so you recommend the place to all the senior girls.

Where's your commission?"

I heard my 3 heroes were writing a book on Clubhouse that would reduce my learning curve and more.

The day the book was released I purchased an eBook and read it that night. It was everything I needed to know to succeed on Clubhouse.

If you want a guidebook on Clubhouse, you can use this link foe easy access   https://bridgingthedigitalgap.com/clubhouse

By now I had been listening to many ways to get ahead in business and I remembered several mentors mentioning "Always be appreciative and show it".

I wanted to show my appreciation to my 3 heroes, so I purchased 50 eBook copies of the book.

I did this in 10 or 20 eBook increments in a few weeks' time.

Knowing what I know now I would have bought them all at the same time so they would have been pushed to best seller faster.

I wasn't sure exactly what I would do with them but there were so many of my friends who had just joined Clubhouse I was hoping to help them as well.

Not to mention, remember I am a Groove Affiliate (even if I forgot) I still had that link on my profiles.

Although, I only got 1 more sale in November, I did get 23 NON-PAID affiliates under me who signed up for the Free Account.

Product Details			Date & Time
Product Name	Price Point	Price	Date Time
GrooveFunnels	11 - GrooveFunnels Free	$0.00	01 Feb 2021 - 10:59 am EST
GrooveFunnels	11 - GrooveFunnels Free	$0.00	01 Feb 2021 - 10:51 am EST
GrooveFunnels	11 - GrooveFunnels Free	$0.00	01 Feb 2021 - 09:46 am EST
GrooveFunnels	11 - GrooveFunnels Free	$0.00	31 Jan 2021 - 04:25 pm EST
GrooveFunnels	11 - GrooveFunnels Free	$0.00	29 Dec 2020 - 10:00 pm EST
GrooveFunnels	11 - GrooveFunnels Free	$0.00	06 Dec 2020 - 11:05 pm EST
GrooveFunnels	11 - GrooveFunnels Free	$0.00	13 Nov 2020 - 05:38 pm EST
GrooveFunnels	11 - GrooveFunnels Free	$0.00	07 Nov 2020 - 09:24 am EST
GrooveFunnels	11 - GrooveFunnels Free	$0.00	05 Nov 2020 - 08:37 am EST
GrooveFunnels	11 - GrooveFunnels Free	$0.00	05 Nov 2020 - 08:32 am EST
GrooveFunnels	11 - GrooveFunnels Free	$0.00	05 Nov 2020 - 07:52 am EST
GrooveFunnels	11 - GrooveFunnels Free	$0.00	05 Nov 2020 - 02:34 am EST
GrooveFunnels	11 - GrooveFunnels Free	$0.00	05 Nov 2020 - 01:55 am EST
GrooveFunnels	11 - GrooveFunnels Free	$0.00	05 Nov 2020 - 12:21 am EST
GrooveFunnels	11 - GrooveFunnels Free	$0.00	04 Nov 2020 - 07:36 pm EST
GrooveFunnels	11 - GrooveFunnels Free	$0.00	04 Nov 2020 - 06:27 pm EST
GrooveFunnels	11 - GrooveFunnels Free	$0.00	04 Nov 2020 - 11:40 am EST
GrooveFunnels	11 - GrooveFunnels Free	$0.00	01 Nov 2020 - 03:54 pm EST
GrooveFunnels	11 - GrooveFunnels Free	$0.00	30 Oct 2020 - 08:02 pm EDT
GrooveFunnels	11 - GrooveFunnels Free	$0.00	28 Oct 2020 - 02:34 am EDT
GrooveFunnels	11 - GrooveFunnels Free	$0.00	24 Oct 2020 - 09:22 pm EDT
GrooveFunnels	11 - GrooveFunnels Free	$0.00	18 Oct 2020 - 10:08 pm EDT

That means if they ever purchase Groove, they would be attached to me, and I would get the commission at the time of purchase. (And this is while I was sleeping again).

So, my 3 heroes, Alicia, Angie & Deb had the train going on zoom/Facebook live a 3rd or 4th time and I was in the comments helping and posting a bit.

When they saw me posting they asked me to join them 'on stage.

NOOOOOOOO!   That is not going to happen.

But I really like and respect them, so I gave in.

That was the beginning of a beautiful friendship and essentially another turning point of my career.

I did what Nick told us (you remember Nick, I am still in the LOF Academy, did I forget to tell you that it was a LIFETIME offer as well), he tells us to:

"Do it Afraid"

Get outside of your comfort zone.

How many times have you heard this from your mentors but never found a scenario to put it into action?

I went a step further as I also went onto Amazon and did a video review for them, I figured no one would know me there. This was officially my first Live/video ever.

We've already established some bullet points on what you can learn from my 3 heroes, but the learning never stops.

Here are a few more Takeaways:

- They tried something that worked, and they repeated it. That's called 'scaling'. I told you I was on the first train. Well weeks later this was happening.
- They were doing 4 trains in one session.
- They were creating posts to get others engaged.
- They were NOT charging anyone for their service.

Clubhouse Conversions

Accelerate your Success On The Hottest NEW Audio Only App

01.07.21 Trains

TRAIN 1 (Support: Jay Patel)	TRAIN 2
12 People From Last Train 12/30/20	✓ Kim Bahr (Gave A New Invite)
✓ Adrian YH (Cont. From Last Week)	✓ Jay Patel
✓ Shannon Stratford	✓ Araje L'Bert
✓ Matt Woosman	✓ John Wheeler
✓ Martina Zorc (Slovenia)	✓ Joella Bower
✓ Olive Oliver (Great Britain)	✓ Fatima Hurd
✓ Ajay Raj (India)	✓ Jennifer Turk
✓ Vinay Chabala (India)	✓ David Sukert (End)
✓ Tracey Rehe (Australia)	
✓ Sandra Ottey (End)	

Hosted By @AliciaLyttle @CoachDeb @AngieNorris

20 Total People	8 Total People
BIG SHOUTOUT to Tonight's ROCKSTAR Support Team: Kisha Fox, Cristine Case, Jay Patel	Facebook Live: 760 Comments

- They were giving shoutouts to the rockstar support Teams

- They documented how many Facebook comments they received

- They showed their appreciation for helpers by calling them out and posting

- They served India, Australia, US, Slovenia etc.....

Join the next trains http://clubhousetrain.com

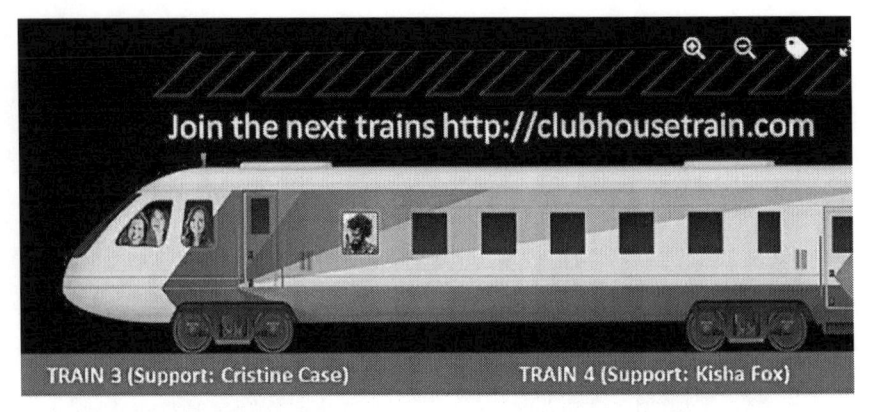

TRAIN 3 (Support: Cristine Case)	TRAIN 4 (Support: Kisha Fox)
14 People From Last 12/30/20	√ Tina Joiner (Gave A New Invite)
/ Ho'olulu Brito (Cont. From Last Week)	√ Bayeck Rebecca
√ Janette Arsenault	√ Dan Hall
√ Sandy England	√ Danielle Hall
√ Richard Gray	√ Andrea Chin (Restart)
√ Dimitra Clark	√ Jill Glascock
√ Cheryl Landfair	√ Victoria Aka
√ Mary Pfeffer	√ Deborah Knight
√ Kim Armstrong	√ Gary Bucher
√ Teri Pitman	√ Michelle Grover
√ Paria Bahar	√ John Gaynor Green (At The Station)
√ Isha Patel (At The Station)	
24 Total People	11 Total People

Tonight's Welcome Team Inside The Clubhouse:
Darcey Hall, Dennis Comstock, Janette Arsenault, Sandy England, Fatima Hurd, Rebecca Bayeck, Jennifer Turk, Tina Joiner

- They had a WELCOME team helping them.

- They were thinking outside the box.

- They did it several nights in a row.

How did I benefit as an affiliate marketer from this experience?

Besides all the free lessons on how to serve others?

- I now had 50 books to give as bonuses
- To give as prizes
- To share with my friends
- To give to my free affiliates. It's not a good idea to have an affiliate if you are going to ignore them Chances are they will never convert.
- I was now on a new platform that went from 100,000 to a million uses in months.
- I was now recognized by my 3 heroes and they in turn mention me on stage often.
- My name is a little connected to each one of them.
- When they have webinars and I show up, they sometimes will announce I am there and tell the clubhouse story of how we met.
- They all consider me a friend and I them.

None of this happened as a 'ploy' to get in their good graces. I was just being authentic and in turn so were they.

Beautiful friendships can come out of relationship building.

Win – Win – Win – Win   God's Way

None of this increased my income at the time. This is what Nick calls 'planting seeds.

Most gardens don't grow over night

But once you plant your seeds and give them love and attention you are bound to see them grow.

After my debut on Facebook Live with my 3 heroes, I still wasn't ready to go introduce myself in a video in Life on Fire Academy, our faith based group.

Now December & January went by, and I hadn't made a penny.

But that didn't stop me from chasing every shiny object I saw.

I was pouring out money but not taking a lot of action.

Are you finding that you get weeks and weeks, or months and months and you just can't get out of your own way?

That was me.

I saw a course online that said, "Make your first Groove Sale in less than 7 days guaranteed".

My eyes went wide open – Groove?

I remember Groove, I made my money back with Groove and then tossed it aside. WHY?

This was a FOUNDER'S COURSE. This course was $7.

I didn't have to borrow the money this time.

MOM & DAD?

The Challenge was taught by Kathy Walls and Rob Verzera.

They said that in 7 days we would be calling them Mom & Dad.

I laughed, I was 62 years old, and I don't call anyone mom & dad anymore.

Well, by day 3, I was calling them mom and dad.

They were awesome.

Their promise was in 7 days 1 Groove sale.

I didn't make that come true but in 10 Days I had 5 sales.

So, I forgive them.

They had class during the day and gave us an assignment. Let me give you an example. In class they taught us how to do a good post on Facebook.

Now I'm thinking, I actually paid money so you can teach me how to type a post on Facebook?

Guess who had a MINDSET problem popping in again.

That's the thing about Mindset.

You don't just learn it once and say Ok, I agree, I will change my mindset.

It is a living breathing 'time bomb' if you let it be.

You can, however, reign it in once you know about it.

As James Malinchak says "First step in Transformation is Awareness"

So, I listened to the class and thought I got the gist of how to do a good post.

The next morning, I did my post and within 5 seconds Rob pops up in my messenger".

> Good morning Joann, Hey great post you just made. Let me ask you a question what can be changed in that post to create more engagement?

I said "Ouch, lol, let me go look" …. "Don't say a video, you know I don't do Live's or video".

"I could have used emojis"

"I could have asked a question at the end".

WINNER!!!!!!!

> Winner!
>
> The post is great and you're telling me a whole bunch of stuff
>
> And then that's it, then you just end. Your post got me thinking about things but didn't tell me to do anything or ask me anything
>
> Post with the purpose to solicit engagement

Winner!

The post is great and you're telling me a whole bunch of stuff

And then that's it, then you just end. Your post got me thinking about things but didn't tll me to do anything or ask me anything

Post with the purpose to solicit engagement!

MIKE DROP!!!!!!!!!!! BOOM!!!!!!!!!!

They are both so down to earth and available to all their students.

Many of us called them mom and dad during the challenge and sometimes when I see them online, I *still* do.

Meet Mom & Dad

You can meet Kathy & Rob by going to:
https://affiliatemarketeronfire.com/kathyandrob

As an Affiliate there are some golden nuggets there.

- Always consider a founder's offer
- Once you post and get people thinking, you need to give them a CTA (call to action).
- Asking a question at the end is the easiest way.
- Putting emoji's in makes the post fun and more people will stop.
- Spacing out the lines will make them easier to read.
- Always post with a purpose to solicit engagement.
- Enjoy learning, it will stick with you longer and be easier to learn.
- Create a relationship with your mentors, it's more fun.

The whole story is just a bit more complicated than just taking a $7 course.

Although the course was great, remember what I said about many courses having bonuses.

One of the bonuses was access to a 21 Day Facebook Challenge.

I can hear Nick Unsworth's voice; "you should go into the group and introduce yourself."

If you want to get noticed faster 'lives' are the way to go.

By now it has been established that I don't do video or Facebook Lives, but…… this was different.

There are so many differently ways to do 'lives', you just need to be creative.

You know that you don't have to use your voice or show your face online to do a 'live'. That's for another day but let that sink in.

You will see that this Challenge was very well planned out.

Each day you are given a different topic.

Once you decide to do your first Facebook live you will begin to see a difference in how long it takes to push the 'live' Button.

The first time I did a 'live' I spent 15 minutes with my hand on the mouse.

It was cramped before I hit go 'live'.

Then, I realized WHY it took me so long.

Do you have any clue what to expect once you hit the Go Live button? I didn't.

I just assumed PRESTO you were on for the whole world to see. **NOT!**

- It opens a screen where you can title your 'live'.
- Then you can put a description.
- You get a camera view so you can see yourself and how you look, and if there is anything in the background you won't want there.
- There are several options you can choose before you hit the button that says, 'GO live'.
- Then this comes up-   3   -   2   -   1
- And then you are 'live'.

This is a picture of my very first Facebook Live in the Challenge. It lasted 59 seconds.

> JoAnn Wolloff was live.
> February 6, 2021
>
> I had to start somewhere, so this 21 Day Challenge is my start

As you can probably guess the next time, I did a live instead of 15 minutes of stalling, I only stalled about 5 minutes.

I still couldn't just jump in, there was much less stall time. Now I have it down to seconds.

There is also a way to do the live and only you can see it. It's in the drop down, change public to only me.

What I would caution you to do is to remember that the **GO LIVE** button turns to **END** after you push it.

I was done with my live and forgot how to get off. Which meant my face was up against the screen reading the whole screen while the world was looking at me.

So, I was nervous when I got off because I didn't know that there is a delete button and an edit button.

What I did find was that as soon as I got off, I had an option to delete the whole thing or just trim it a bit.

Some Key points to remember:

- Know your opening statement before hitting Go Live
- Know what you are going to say to get off
- Start with under 5 minutes, 2-3 are great beginner Lives.
- Remember to check the camera not only at your appearance (I was ready to hit live once, and I was still in pj's). Also, look around you for things hanging on furniture or stuff you just don't want broadcast to the world.
- Remember the same place you hit Go Live will be END when you are finished.
- Remember to have fun.
- Remember to laugh if you make a mistake and acknowledge you are nervous
- You are able to trim off the very uncomfortable ending.

Everyone must do their first Live sometime and we all remember what it was like. So let them know you are a Facebook Live Newbie.

You will be amazed at how people soften right up when they see someone being vulnerable.

If you want to try the 21 Day Facebook Challenge free download at https://affiliatemarketeronfire.com/fblive

"You might be an Affiliate If...
...you see a baseball scout hanging around and he is scouting the wrong person, so you clue him in on the good talent.

Where's your commission?"

Does doing social media help an Affiliate Marketer?

Once I started doing Facebook Lives, my first few were awkward but received nicely by everyone.

I followed the daily schedule and one day I mentioned my parents.

That same day I received a message from my babysitter.

I am 62 years old and the women who was there the day I came home from the hospital reached out to me to tell me how many memories this post brought back to her.

I didn't even remember we were friends on Facebook.

Who knows how long ago we connected?

I know I had never, ever seen her comment on even one of my posts.... until now that I did a Facebook LIVE.

How many times do you post something and because no one put a comment in your post you assume no one saw it?

WRONG!

Let me give you another example:

My husband's, 2nd cousin's husband, Todd signed up to a Free Groove account because one of them saw my FB Live.

One of the topics is to bring up what you do.

We hadn't seen or heard from them in almost 20 years. Now he is one of my affiliates in my new business.

Facebook Lives or Reels, or YouTube, or TikTok can all have the same effect.

You would approach them all a little differently but once you pick that platform, you learn it till it comes naturally and effortlessly.

Once you are comfortable with your platform you can add another one.

Overwhelm comes when you try to do to many things at once that all require a learning curve.

Having multiple streams of income is great but secure one first.

"You might be an Affiliate If…
…you stay at a great hotel, and they have free buffet, that's where you tell everyone to stay

Where's your commission?"

Who watches your Facebook Lives?

The last time I saw my brother Bob, he jokingly said to me "Can I get your autograph?".

I hadn't seen him in a year or heard from him on Facebook but evidently, he was watching my page.

PEOPLE ARE WATCHING

I had recently received an award for 'Affiliate of the Year' from one of my mentors and he was kidding me about it.

He said he didn't understand what it was. But he was happy for me. He gets MLM mixed up with Affiliate Marketing.

There is a world of difference between them but there are so many people who don't know that difference yet.

Let's jump back to Angie Norris for a minute.

One day Angie puts out a post that said "Does anyone live in the Tampa Bay area. I will be in town and would love to meet up"

(That's not exactly the wording, but close enough.)

Would you like to meet someone who was in your field and made $30,000 in one month? I would.

Angie and her husband came to town. There were about 15 of us who were local and took her up on her invite.

I brought my husband, Win and that was huge. Until now he was a 'skeptic'. (He took this picture).

Not a naysayer but a 'I'll believe it when I see it kind'.

Trying to be supportive but not quite understanding and had a very suspicious mind.

How many of you are in that same exact place?

You have a spouse or grown-up kids or friends who love you, but they don't really believe this will work for you.

So, you start taking on their beliefs and eventually you quit.

Can you say, 'MINDSET adjustment'.

We all know where that will lead you by now.

You need to trust that you have your eyes wide open and be careful about the 'shiny objects and scams'.

But just because your loved one doesn't believe doesn't mean they are right.

Believe in yourself.

The meetup was a huge success.

My husband was now on board 100% and things made more sense to him now.

He loved meeting everyone and liked all of them.

He realized they were all like me just trying to find out what niche we want to be in and the best way to continue.

During one of my conversations with 'the bigger than life' Angie Norris (that was my impression of her success) she was one of my heroes already, I got complete clarity.

She told me how she had the Imposter Syndrome big time.

Even with all her success and she was doing well in the corporate world before this, she still felt like an imposter most of the time.

She said "Jo-Ann, I can't believe all of you came out here to meet me tonight. This is crazy". She was so humble and authentic, I was floored.

A Few Affiliate Tips:

- You should follow someone who is already making it in your field.
- Take advantage of meeting them if the opportunity arises.
- Post in your groups when you are going to be in another town, offer to meetup with like-minded people.
- Imposter Syndrome is a real thing. But it does not need to affect you negatively. You will learn what others already know, that you are worth it.
- Take pictures with everyone. You never know if they will be great friends someday and you will want that first time you met picture. (Or is that just me, I'm married to a professional photographer)

This was our very first meeting and the beginning of a very special friendship.

To check out Angie go to:
https://affiliatemarketeronfire.com/angie

MONEY FLOW

How Do You Make Money?

One of the major things I found out was that when you have a product and that company plans promotions, you make sure to be geared up when the next promotion comes.

With that being said, I always knew when Groove was doing a promotion and I was ready.

March was the first month I made over 5 figures in one month.

Does this Facebook cover design look familiar?

Remember the journey I was taking my Facebook friends on.

The idea is to change your cover which helps keep you accountable.

Everyone has their own system on what they do during promotion time.

Depending on the company you are promoting, you want to be aware at least a week or two before the promo is about to start.

Many companies like Groove will help you promote.

- They offer you different scripts to send out in your email.
- They will offer you different posts to put on your social media pages
- They will write out blog posts for you to use
- They will create banners for you
- They may run a contest for the highest achievers.

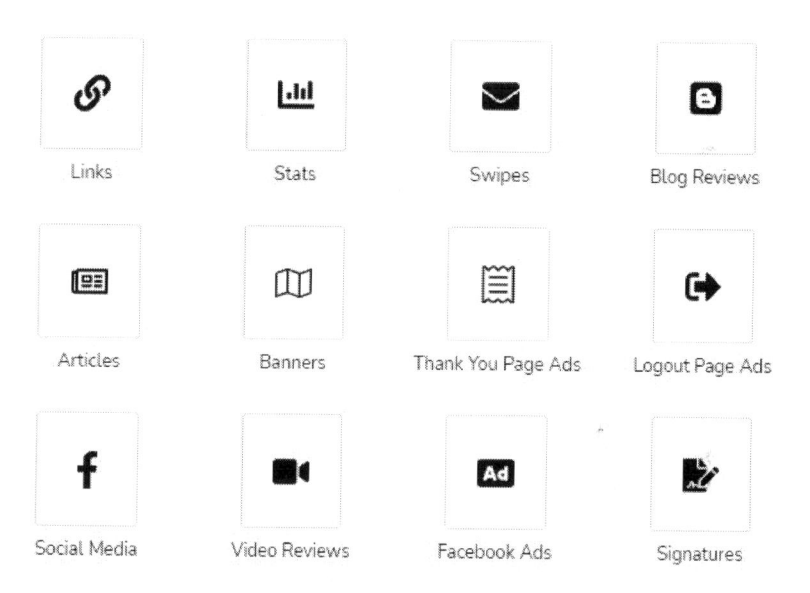

Links	Stats	Swipes	Blog Reviews
Articles	Banners	Thank You Page Ads	Logout Page Ads
Social Media	Video Reviews	Facebook Ads	Signatures

I'm not fond of competition so these contests are not usually fun for me.

With that said I have been on the leader board 4 times in the last 4 promotions.

The first 3 times it was by accident that I was on. I did not have a full-blown promotion to launch.

However, by the 4th promotion, it was GAME ON.

Which means I had planted enough seeds that when Groove kicked off their promotions and their bonuses my free affiliates decided to upgrade.

Which in turn put me on the leader board.

Groove always does long promotions so I had time to get prepared for by the time the first 3 promos finished, and I was able to make money on each of them, but I would recommend that you be prepared at least 1 week before your product does a promo kick off.

Otherwise, the whole promotion week you don't sleep much.

During promotion week you want to triple your lives, your webinars, your demo's anything to do with that product.

Remember the Facebook cover rule. You want to keep your Facebook friends updated during the journey.

I didn't update my Facebook cover every single time I made a sale. I waited a month or so to do the update.

Do you make sure to celebrate your win's?

It is extremely important to celebrate. In the LOF Academy we have Wins day (instead of Wednesday). Every Wednesday you are encouraged to show something you are celebrating.

Also, at the beginning of every month you should not only be declaring your goals, but you should also be posting them publicly.

Sometimes life just swallows you up and you get derailed. I stopped posting the Fb Cover's at 29X's.

If I were to do it today, it would read 96X's (sales)

[Figure: thought-bubble collage showing sales across many dates — 1X's in Jan 2022, 1X's in March 2022, 1X's in May 2022, 15X's in Feb 2022, This Happened Nov 4, Nov 7, Nov 11 & Nov 23, 2020, Feb 23, 24, 25 and 2X's on the 28th 2021, 4X's on March 10th 2021, 5X's in May 2021, 3 X's on March 8th and 16th 2021, March 23rd, 4X's on March 17th 2021, 8X's in July 2021, 2X's in June 2021, 6X's in Oct 2021, March 28 2021, 1X's in Nov 2021, 9X's in Aug 2021, 2X's on April 2nd 2021, 2X's on April 2nd 2021, 8X's in Sept 2021, 5X's in Dec 2021, "Congratulations! You've made a sale as an affiliate. Product —, Sale Amount: $1397.00, Your commission: $558.80", "96X's and counting", "NO BRAINER!", "And 5 Asst", "Click Here to see how this can happen to you!"]

This made it fun for my friends and family to follow along and of course for new people to say: **"What's Groove?" (Or whatever your product is)**

Remember you pick up new friends all the time and they should know what you do.

Once you have a product, as you can tell by now, I have a solid product.

I use Groove as a website, an opt-in page and sales page.

I make my money by being a Groove affiliate selling Groove itself. But I wanted more....

Once you find a product, the ideal solution is to find another product or service that complements the one you have.

This does 2 things.

- It gives you another potential income source
- It lets you keep your same clients without constantly having to make new lists.

If my products complement each other than someone using one of the products may really like or need the second product, so I am doing them a favor or a service.

If you are offering a website platform, and it doesn't matter if it is Groove, or Kajabi, or ClickFunnels it can be any platform you are comfortable with, (just make sure they have an affiliate program) it makes sense to offer a "Do it with you" service or a "Do it for you" service.

You could also offer classes to teach them how to use the product.

You could offer to do it for them as well.

You could offer other people's courses and take an affiliate percentage from their profit. Sub-Affiliates are quite common.

Using your main Website builder as your base product, you could ask what other products might these same users need?

Once You figure it out, you would offer the solution to these needs as your complementary products.

For a FREE list of products that complement website platforms (any platform) go to:
https://affiliatemarketeronfire.com/complementary

"You might be an Affiliate If…

… *your tv broke and you went to Walmart and picked up another tv that is so much better than the one you had that you bragged to anyone who would listen.*

Where's your commission?

IS EXPERIENCE NEEDED?

Do You Have to Be TECHY?

Many of my coaching clients are not 'techy'.

Did you know that 'techy' is a state of mind or MINDSET?

It just means there is a process or procedure you haven't learned yet.

The best thing you can do when you learn something new is to use it and then teach it to someone else.

That will re-enforce it much quicker in your mind.

I tell my students in my membership "If you learned one thing at a time in the 'techy world' and did only one a day, you would have 30 new skills at the end of the first month."

Anyone can do that. Do not label yourself 'not techy'. How about **"tech in training'**

Being creative is half the battle. There are no set rules you need to live by, if you are fair and honest, the sky is the limit.

Remember we are doing it so that everyone gets a Win-Win God's Way.

"I am a TECH IN TRAINING"

Photo Shoot

How often do you need to put your picture online?

One way to be creative and look Techy

Do you have any recent photos?

Do you have all headshots looking straight forward and arms down by your side?

I am a little luckier than most as I have been married to a professional photographer, Win Wolloff, for the last 40 years.

This means that I not only don't pay for photos, but I get to have them at any time I want.

But that would make me the exception.

You have the option of going to a professional or using your own cell phone.

The new iPhone is incredible.

The main reason I bring up pictures is that you need to be Intentional with your shoot.

Whether it is a friend doing it, selfies on a tripod or a professional.

What should you shoot?

- Take different shirt tops, white, black, colors
- Take full length, headshots, action shots
- Take shots with your head looking in all directions
- Take shots pointing up, down, sideways
- Take shots with you pretending to hold something.
- Take shots with a surprise look on your face,
- A look of shock, or relief

WHY? Because you are now on the internet. If you use the same 3 pictures every time you make an ad or promote a product you will be disappointed.

However, if you can use a variety of poses and expressions your options will be limitless.

So basically, all you did was set your phone on a tripod and make goofy faces and some good faces and you are now considered Techy. You put a little thought into it. You now have plenty of options for your posts.

Look up professional sites to get ideas, you could start with my husband's site (see how shamelessly I promoted him, now you know why we have been married so long).

Go to: https://affiliatemarketeronfire.com/win

A side story on how me met. We met in 1980 at a roller-skating rink, when his 4-year-old daughter Kate said "Daddy, this is my friend Jo-Ann."

To that he said, "I know your friend Jo-Ann, I took her senior class pictures 4 years ago."

Now I'm thinking, there's a line I haven't heard. He went on "we talked about karate". WINNER!!!!!!!

We did. My dad was a blue belt, some of brothers were blackbelts, my sister Jeanne and I were brown belts in Tae-Kwon-Do.

He took my senior picture in 1976. Talk about planting seeds. People remember more than you think.

How Do You Get a Tribe?

Here are some ninja tips on how to slip into someone's space without invading their space.

We all receive notices about friends' birthdays.

Facebook uses the term friends very loosely.

We need to remember these are first acquaintances whose trust you must gain to call them friends.

I have at least 6-10 friends with birthdays every single day (according to Facebook).

Let me tell you about a habit that takes very little effort and produces great rewards.

On November 30, 2020, I turned 63.

I was watching Facebook because I love reading my birthday messages each year.

This year I decided that I would not only read my messages but also answer each one.

Although, I started later in the day, it seemed like a fun way to celebrate my birthday.

Little did I know that four days later I would still be answering happy birthday messages.

Think about it, we not only get birthday messages from our family and close friends but these new Facebook Friends/acquaintances as well.

It was easy when it was someone I knew, but what do you say to the people who you don't know or never met before besides happy birthday on their birthday.

I found I wanted to know them better.

They took the time out of their day to say happy birthday to me and I wanted to give them the same consideration.

So, if I did not know them, I went to their Facebook pages and looked at their profiles. This was eye opening.

I would answer an acquaintances HAPPY BIRTHDAY with "thank you very much Sandy, I had a wonderful birthday. I was checking out your page and realized we are in the same business, I love that. Thanks again for the birthday wishes".

Or "thank you for the warm wishes, I didn't realize you lived in Florida too, cool coincidence." "Are you a native?"

Or "thank you for thinking of me, I always love this day because I get to meet so many friendly people all wishing me well."

"Doesn't get any better than this does it?"

As you can see each of these responses and there are hundreds of other responses that you could reply with are an opener for the other person to write back.

The idea is to answer them with something familiar to them. Preferably something they might want to expand on.

Now you will have a personality to put to the name. You might have a conversation started.

Yes, this does take a long time. Which is why I make sure that instead of answering each one on my birthday wishes, I switch it around and do their birthdays instead.

This little birthday bear sings Happy Birthday and some of my new friends were getting a quick video too.

Daily now, I will look at whose birthday it is and then I only have 6-10 people to send birthday wishes to.

But I would look at their profile first if I didn't already know them, and many times, I find we have things in common, so I add a personal comment to my birthday wish.

"Happy Birthday Sue, I hope you get to spend some time with those beautiful grandchildren I saw on your page recently."
Be authentic.

You are not likely to find people in a better mood then on their birthday receiving good wishes from everyone. A great time to make their acquaintance.

Notice I didn't say "Sell to them".

We are creating relationships.

Affiliate marketing is mostly started with relationships. There are places like Amazon, Clickbanks and other Marketplaces but for this book we will talk organic.

I realize there are apps out there that you can automate. But remember why you are doing this exercise; you are trying to form an initial bond.

I'm afraid people can see a 'bot' birthday from a mile away. Yes, I appreciate the birthday wish, but it is not going to go out to your profile to get something personal about you. This is for scaling mostly.

That must be programmed into the bot ahead of time.

So, leave the birthday bot for when you have a solid list, and you are ready to scale.

Or you already have all the personal info, and you can load the bot.

Groovy-Jo Bot   Groove Tech Queen

I like bots. I have my own. I call her Groovy-Jo Bot.

Bots can really scale your business, but you must have a plan first and be willing to learn and take action.

If bot's interests you, I can point you in the right direction just go to https://affiliatemarketeronfire.com/bots

Takeaways:

- This can take a few minutes out of your day every day so it should be time blocked. Ex: 10 minutes at 8:00 every morning happy birthday habit.

- Noon every day, see if anyone on Facebook has replied to any of your posts.

- Keep the birthday wishes short and uplifting.

- Anytime you mention children or recreational vehicles you are bound to get a reply.

- The way Facebook works, once you answer someone's comment you are more than likely to see many more of their posts for a few weeks.

- Intentionally turn this into a habit.

This will bring a lot more people into your view and you will be in their view as well.

Facebook, Instagram, YouTube and TikTok love to see more engagement and in turn they will show your posts to more people.

It's a great way to extend your reach.

"You might be an Affiliate If…

…you like the way your grass looks this week, and you recommend the maintenance company to your neighbors

Where's your commission?"

Join as many Groups as you can.

This may be Facebook/social media or in person groups, there are plenty of both.

When talking about online groups:

- Go back to the first assignment in this book where you stopped and wrote down things you are passionate about.
- Or things you could share with others.
- Go to Groups - in the Search type your passion.

Hundreds of groups might show up. Be particular. You don't want spammy groups, where anything goes. Meaning every other post is a sale of some sort daily.

Joining groups is very important.

Writing a post is a great start to break the ice.

- You can post a quote.
- A joke,
- A passage of Scripture
- A poem.
- You could do a live
- You can just answer other people's questions.
- Or you can do all the above and get a jump start.
- The trick is to be consistent.
- You can't just post once and think it will do the job.

Online recognition will take time. The more you give of yourself the faster it will go.

"You might be an Affiliate If…

… you saw a new TV Show last night and can't get it off your mind and you find yourself asking if others saw it? You proceed to tell them what night it's on and such.
Where's your commission?"

Many groups allow what's called a promotion day one day a week they allow you to promote in their group.

Meaning one day a week you can post your offer without slamming them.

When you get into these groups, make friends fast so that on promotion day your offer will hit more people's view.

Remember to show some interests in others' post.

Ask questions in their threads.

Keep the conversation going so you can come back occasionally, and post on it.

This does NOT mean you stay online all day. NOOOOOOO That is the last thing you want to do.

Many new entrepreneurs spend entirely too much time online because they caught up in the drama.

Stay away from the drama.

If getting ahead is truly what you want, then you should only be reading and answering posts that will jumpstart you in that direction.

Family posts are great but only when they are uplifting. Do not go down other people's rabbit holes.

Don't let them set up your day. Read, Post, get on to profit producing activities

Have you heard the word Influencer around the digital world?

I am sure you have seen them, but do you know how they got to be an influencer?

I am guessing they started with 'lives' whether it was Facebook Live or YouTube or Instagram reels or even the newest one TikTok.

Earlier I told you how I started with Facebook Lives, now let's touch upon how I started with YouTube. (It wasn't a pretty sight!)

I started my YouTube 'career' and I use that term very loosely, but as you must have guessed, I made every mistake in the book.

But I don't call them mistakes anymore. They were all a part of my education.

They were just learning steps along the way.

Now is a good time to introduce you to my 3rd Hero officially. Coach Deb or Deb Cole.

"You might be an Affiliate If...
...you give use a wedding planner for your wedding and there wasn't a single hitch, now this is the only wedding planner that exists in your world.

Where's your commission?"

Influencers

I had already seen CoachDeb on plenty of occasions, so she didn't have to earn my 'know, like or trust.' She was already one of my 3 Heroes.

What you don't know about CoachDeb is that she was once a producer for Larry King. She was also a talk show host. Which is only a small part of her career.

I was watching another SUMMIT and CoachDeb had a program and after watching her demo, it really didn't matter what she was selling, I was all in.

Of course, CoachDeb 10 years ago learned from Alicia Lyttle, so you know that marketing is a very strong asset for her as well.

The course was 'Social Video Marketing'.

You might be thinking, 'Jo-Ann has veered off course again. Les Brown has a pet squirrel (in his mind) and he's constantly talking to him as if he was on the side of him. He named him Tyrone. I love it.
Anyone who follows Les will know his squirrel's name.

Les has taken the Tyrone scenario even further.

Recently, I caught a Facebook Live from Les, and he has given Tyrone (his pretend squirrel) a girlfriend. I have to make a point to ask her name. He said it but I was laughing too hard. It was a hoot! I love this guy!

Talk about taking people on your journey with you.
You can read more about Les here
https://bridgingthedigitalgap.com/les

This man is a Legend

"You might be an Affiliate If...
...you get a manicure, pedicure and is over the moon at the results so of course you tell everyone.

Where's your commission?

Lesson here:

Tell your story and bring people on your journey and have fun with it! Ok. This time, I did take you off track, back on track now.
How did my knowing CoachDeb help me?

A better question to ask might be, what's this got to do with affiliate marketing and how can it help you?

Remember, I told you I thought I did it all wrong. That's not accurate. I didn't do it right the first time, but that did not make it wrong.

Nick & Megan have a saying: **"Done Beats Perfect"**.

So, I trusted them and guess what? I'm still here, and things are so much easier now.

If I hadn't gotten started, I would not have gotten all of that learning behind me.

My product (Groove) was having a 'Groove-a-thon'. Replace Groove in your story for any product of yours.

Groove would teach their software for what I believe was 12 days. Six- eight hours a day.

During the teaching they would make an offer.

I mentioned earlier that if your product is going to do a promotion, **you must be ready to promote** when they do.

I was having some success in affiliate marketing, and I wanted to share it with everyone.

I had this great idea that I would give out **Free short tips on Affiliate Marketing during the Groove-a-thon.**

Did you ever want something so badly that you go all in and overdo it and totally overwhelm yourself?

So far that seems harmless, right?
Now comes the How. How would I deliver these tips alongside of the Groove-a-thon?

Common sense says since I am pretty comfortable with **Facebook Lives,** so I could start there.

https://www.facebook.com/joann.wolloff/

Whenever my product promotes, I make money, so I wanted to up my game and I decided I will also do **Instagram Reels.**

(I had done only 2 or 3 reels ever).

https://www.instagram.com/joannwolloff/

Since I had the video's, I thought that **YouTube** was my next logical step (after all, I did go to a 2-day summit once where they showed me how to set up my YouTube channel so that I could do my first post).

https://www.youtube.com/channel/UCyVIIBK6PjgmQRtnnIQLQrg

Finally, I heard about this thing called **TikTok.**
(I had gone to a 60-minute webinar about TikTok last month so I should be able to handle it right?)

https://www.tiktok.com/@joannwolloff?lang=en

https://www.linkedin.com/in/joann-wolloff-b52a6642/ Don't forget LinkedIN either. All these thoughts went through my poor brain in a single morning.

        Do you see this train derailing quickly?
            Can you say **Train Wreck!**

But Wait There's More!
(Wow twice in one book)

Did I mention how often I was going to do these tips?
I know the most obvious would be once a day for the 12 days.

NOT ME, this overachiever somehow thought that every hour of the Groove-a-thon should have its own tip.

Doing the math that's over 70 tips on four platforms many of them live.

I work from home and sometimes the two worlds are not separated enough.

I post from my office (which doubles as my living room, which never looks the same.)

Sometimes when I post it looked like 'a workday in progress'. Which is a nice way of saying a 'disaster'.

I was not conscious of my background when doing my YouTube videos.

At any given time, I could have had my bathrobe draped over the couch, or my breakfast plate placed behind me for the next time I walked into the kitchen.

On several occasions my husband walked in behind me while I was talking.

Which of course when you are a newbie, you totally lose track of what you are saying, and you are LIVE.

I actually got flustered and upset at him while I was LIVE (hello!)

I am just being real here. The best thing about 'lives' is you do get a chance to delete them.
Later, you will see how my growing in 'lives' changed my whole attitude.

I literally made myself sick during these 12 days.

My blood pressure went through the roof.

Has this happened to you? Try to do too much? What did you do?

You might be an Affiliate If…

… you took golf lessons recently and now your game has totally improved and everyone on the course knows why.

Where's your commission?"

Here is what my lives/reels/video/TikTok's looked like

Day 4 tip #25 Join Online Affiliate Groups Groove.mp4

Cut Tip-a-thon update.mp4

GMT20210419-205932_Recording_avo_1280x720.mp4

Day4 # 26 Local Neighborhood Next Door.mp4

Day 4 # 25 Not Glued to One Platform.mp4

Cut Tip A Thon.mp4

Day 3 Tip 17 Meet new people using Birthdays.mp4

Day 2 tip 16 Opt-In Page.mp4

Day 2 Tip 15 Follow up.mp4

day 7 tip 52.MOV

day 7 tip 51.MOV

day 7 tip 50.MOV

Notice there are no preselected thumbnails. Any clip was used as the thumbnail.

What can you learn from my adventures?

LET ME COUNT THE WAYS:

- Use a thumbnail (instead of the odd shots from the video)

- Have a background promoting my items

- Wear a logo on your hat or shirt

- Have a consistent naming convention

- Don't go on platforms I know virtually nothing about

- Don't do four platforms at one time with no experience

- Use a scheduling tool for the posts

- Don't drop platforms (no consistency)

- Don't miss hours at a time (keep my word)

- Take better care of your health

- Form better habits

In fact, one of my 'habits' is to help keep my Life on Fire Family accountable.
I do that by making sure they don't miss the scheduled sessions weekly.

Accountability

One morning, I was so excited about class that I did a 'FB live' first thing in the morning (before getting out of my flannel PJ's).

One of the comments was "I love your Christmas PJ's".

A lightbulb went off. I decided that was my 'hook'.

I would wear the same PJ top every single time they had a class. It got so they just saw me on and knew there was a class that day.

So that works for the Life on Fire Regular Sessions. We have now been through 5 versions and the PJ's still come out.

I have also joined other courses with this group, and I wanted to keep them accountable for these classes without getting them confused.

Watch the backgrounds, see how much I have learned.
For Speaker on Fire, I wore a long sleeve blue work shirt, and I had a microphone in my hands when I reminded them, they had a class in a few hours.

A few times during the week I would do a live when there wasn't a class (no blue shirt or mike) and I would try to be 'intentional' no blue shirt or mike not a class day.

That is something most people do wrong.

You don't just come on live and show your lunch every day unless there is a purpose to that lunch. Say it was a new restaurant. That would be intentional.

But many people are just going live to go live and that is not going to help as much as being 'intentional'

You've all seen promotions where entrepreneurs would promote their product using their children.

There are mixed views here, but I tend to think if you do it naturally and tastefully it can be a lot of fun (for everyone).

Let's face it we all love to see the antics of kids. It naturally puts a smile on our faces.

For instance, I was playing with Reagan and Maverick (2 of my precious grandchildren) one day and they were supposed to be hiding in the room, waiting for me.

I decided to do a quick live and they snuck up on me and were waving in the back of my chair.

It was priceless. Here I am saying "don't tell the kids I am online, and they are behind me".

Some people would say that is 'unprofessional'.

If you have learned anything from this book, please "DON'T LISTEN TO THE NAYSAYER'S".

Did it make you and the kids happy? That is all that counts. This is your life, live every day of it the way you want to. Making money doesn't mean you have to be miserable. Have fun.

"You might be an Affiliate If...

... your friend wrote a book, and you think everyone should read it.

Where's your commission?"

How can knowing about the kids help you?

- It's ok to not be perfect on screen
- It's good to pull people into your lifestyle so they can identify with you.
- You can be professional or intentional both work.
- This is your LIFE; you don't turn off your life to do your business. You are who you are, when you need to separate them, you will, but that will be your choice.

Getting back to the Accountability habits, for Best Seller on Fire, I heard James say that he wanted us to get up and move around and be awake for the class.

I did a few jumping jacks before each class and did them live to remind everyone of the class.

The day of the 5th class, Reagan and Maverick were here overnight. I asked them to join me in my jumping jacks.

Although, we reminded everyone about the class, I skipped the class & caught the replay.

Because as my husband (Win) loves to repeat from his grandfather (Orin B. Ellison),

"If the kids interfere with the Business, give up the Business".

The point I am getting at Is -

WHY DID YOU DECIDE TO BECOME AN ENTREPRENEUR?

Was it because you wanted to spend more time with your FAMILY maybe?

So now I have my priorities straight, what about my background?

Instead of being unaware of my surroundings, I started being intentional about what should show up in the Video.

For instance, instead of a picture of a group no one knows on the wall, I hung my awards and my new best seller "Affiliate Marketer on Fire"

I hung my Groove light. I lite it every time I went online. I have my website so it can be seen when I am on zoom calls.

Remember, this is one of my products.

Do you have any of your products that can be used as props. I keep some on the desk to be used online at any moment.

I hung the Kingdom Impact Awards I have earned.

I would wear a shirt or sweater from one of the products I love.

Would you like an Unsworth Angel shirt? Go to:
https://affiliatemarketeronfire.com/angelshirt

If it is an outdoor shot, I would wear one of my visors with a logo I am promoting. Even if you never mention the hat, it's in the Video the whole time so it will be noticed

Always celebrate your wins

During the Groove-a-thon I made over 5 figures, even if I was all over the place with my promotional platforms and my backgrounds.

I would go into Canva or now-a-days Clickdesigns and create a quick post and on Wins Day post something like this.

Clickdesigns is my newest and most exciting addition to my affiliate marketing tools.

If I had to explain it quickly, I would say it is Canva on steroids.

- Always celebrate your affiliate win's
- Post a question to see if anyone wants to learn how to do this.
- Put an address where they could reach you if they wanted to be notified of your next webinar.

These are all small little seeds you drop along your affiliate journey.

You will notice that I didn't do any one thing to make all these sales in under a year. I planted seeds and nurtured them and watch them grow.

People must know what you do to use your offer.

Make it easy for them and leave them links or email addresses right there so they can highlight or jot it down.

But be careful. Throwing your links in people's faces is NOT what I am suggesting.

These are just simple ways to 'Tell' people about your products and services without "Selling" people.

I picked up these hacks, and many more from a Social Video Bootcamp taught by CoachDeb (whose class I am currently still in).

Being live in videos and Reels is currently the hottest platform, and it's important to stay on top of small pieces of info like that.

Recently, I was helping another entrepreneur find affiliate products that bring in larger commissions.

He is a newbie, and all his commissions are on the low side.

You might be an Affiliate If...

...you found a new carwash that does an excellent detailing job. Who did you tell?

Where's your commission?

"Specifically, he asked "How would I get my diabetes client to buy something else from me?" I asked him to think about his client. Whoever your client is for your actual product they may be an entrepreneur or could need a design tool.

They may own a business.

They may also, know someone who is in business, and you could ask them for names.

I suggested some of my higher paying commission products (a few already mentioned in this book) so he would have a start.

They could need a webpage.

They could be a company that has w2 employees and didn't get the whole rebate the government was offering (more later)

The possibilities are endless.

Clients for one item will absolutely be your client for another item when you have your eyes open as an affiliate.

Since they already, know, like and trust you they would welcome suggestions on how to make their lives easier.

This week's Social Video class was on Instagram Reels/Templates, Music and Pure Gold.

If you want some more free hacks to download or more info on CoachDeb's bootcamp, go to
https://affiliatemarketeronfire.com/coachdeb

"You might be an Affiliate If...
...you go bowling and find out they have a special several days a week, who you going to tell, you know you will tell someone.

Where's your commission?"

It's only fitting I take this opportunity to tell you why I am writing this book and who is to 'blame'

That would be James Malinchak- **Featured on ABC's Hit TV Show, "Secret Millionaire"** along with Nick Unsworth **CEO of Life on Fire** and Megan Unsworth the '**First Lady of Life on Fire**" and the **Queen of Coaching**.

A free challenge called Speaker on Fire came across my desk.

By now you know these 3 mentors, Nick Unsworth, James Malinchak, and Megan Unsworth.

Since I was studying how to do YouTube and Facebook Lives this seems like a natural progression.

Remember Bonuses.... Of all the bonuses that I ever had offered to me when I purchased a product **THE bonus given to us from Speaker on Fire was** by far my **#1 favorite.**

This was one of those instances like with CoachDeb, and with Alicia Lyttle or Angie Norris, I didn't care what the product was because I know, like, and trust them and the bonuses overshadowed the product.

Although, speaking in public is in my future the main reason I signed up was for the bonuses.

I'm sure you are wondering what kind of bonus would get me this excited.

There were several bonuses but the one I am referring to is what I thought was a 2-day Free convention.

What would you think of a Free 2-day convention?

I know, I know, we get conventions thrown in more and more these days so that shouldn't have me so excited. **It doesn't.**

This convention is limited to fifteen students (including our guest we were allowed to bring).

When was the last time you were at a convention with these odds of spending quality time with the instructor?

This convention, which I found out is not really a convention after all, it is a Private 2-Day Group Coaching & Mastermind taught by James himself.

"You might be an Affiliate If...
...you get really cheap airline tickets & you boast about it on social media
Where's your commission?"

"But wait there's more!"

It was held at his Las Vegas mansion.
(Did you catch that, in his HOME in Las Vegas).

The speaker course might have been on how to speak in public, but the bonus instructions said:

> *From now until you meet with James, keep a small with notebook you at all times and write down any/every comes question to that mind about speaking, writing, coaching, running business, a platform selling, branding, marketing, selling yourself, structuring a business, making money, etc.
>
> This is your day with James and he will answer any of your business-related questions and will help you with any business- related areas.
>
> Remember, James is an authority on how to market and make money with any type of business so feel free to ask any questions whatsoever".

This is a $25,000 value and I received it as a bonus because I wasn't afraid to resource up at the right time.

"You might be an Affiliate If...
... you wrote a book and mentioned a webinar you want to and highly recommend it.

Where's your commission?"

This was our group

These instructions are relevant to all of us:

- Always keep a small notebook with you
- Write down every question you have about anything
- When you get into a class where they allow questions you already have them written down

During the Speaker on Fire Course, one of the most important areas I got clarity on was how critical it is to write a book.

Seems odd, doesn't it? That my major Ah-ha moment for speaker on fire is that I should write a book asap.

I know this is a long way to get to a point, but if you hang in there you will see what all this means to you as an affiliate marketer.

The course was on speaking. This book is on affiliate marketing yet both speakers and affiliate marketers would have a huge jumpstart to their careers if they considered writing that first book. Why?

By now I am pretty good at knowing which shiny objects will sit on a shelf and which are directly related to what I am doing currently, so I know when it's time to resource up.

The same creators created another free challenge a few months later. It was called Best Seller on Fire and it came across my desk. BRILLIANT!

Since I had learned in the previous challenge how important writing a book could be for taking your career to the next level, this seemed like a natural progression.

Or as I like to say a "no brainer'.

As you can tell the organizers of the challenge really know how to market their product.

They saw a problem and offered a solution.

They knew there would be a need for a book writing course as most every mentor right now is teaching this same concept.

How do I write, produce, and market my book? What do I write my book on, I don't have a product I am an affiliate?

They didn't just get us all excited in Speaker on Fire about writing a book, they then gave us a way to learn how to write it and what to use it for. Be the Solution! That's key.

That's Key!

Have you looked up James yet, check out his offers:
https://bridgingthedigitalgap.com/jamesm

If you notice the book title, it says it all. 'Success Starts with Attitude'.

Have you looked up James yet, check out some of his books? https://bridgingthedigitalgap.com/james

Story behind this picture. James was signing autographs for everyone who bought the book. I was standing in the long line for my turn.

Earlier I was a part of the team helping to move people through the lines and such.

James and I locked eyes for a second and I said, "Bet you wish I was helping now" He laughed and said "Yeah".

A few minutes later, there was a tap on my shoulder "Jo-Ann I really meant it, I wouldn't mind your help."

Lol, it took me less than a split second to jump out of line and move that line along.

Write a Book

How can writing a book help? A book is the new 'Business Card'. It opens doors that would never have been open to you before.

    Recently, two of my grandkids were over and I was showing them my book when my 9 yr old granddaughter said "I wrote a book once for school"?

I had no idea. She went home and found the book, texted me the title and I found it online and purchased it. The second grade at her school did a collaborative book where they each got one page.

Do you remember at the front of this book where I was on a collaborative book with my peers.

It seems my granddaughter had beat me to being a Published Author, when she was only 8 years old.

Give me a little leeway while I celebrate my granddaughter.

The book was titled OUR GIFTS TO THE WORLD : Did you know people have gifts to the world? one of my gifts to the world is kindness. Kindness makes people comfortable. Another gift to the world is Smartness. Smartness helps me do school work and helps me solve problems. Something else I am good at is being silly. This makes people laugh and be happy. Another talent I have is remeoring things. If someone forgets something I tell them what they forgot. A talent I have is Love. Love can mean caring for something or someone. Everyone has a talent or gift to the world. p.s. people can have multiple gifts to the world. Reagan
    To: Meme From:Reagan

You know I had to get it autographed and celebrate her.

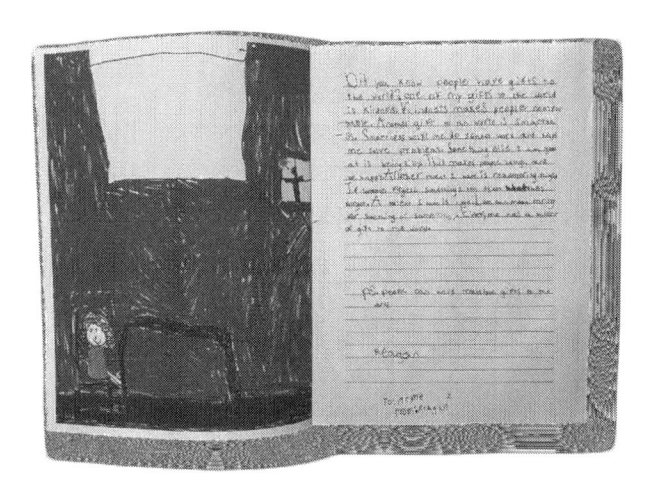

Her brother Maverick and I did a bunch of goofy photo's with her but we did manage to get this one.

Writing the book can be fast and short (like Reagan's book) or take a long time and put some personal experiences in it. Either way it is a must these days to have a book.

If you actually have a product or service, the ideal book to write is about your service arena or product uses or origination.

This way you have even more options with the book.

Besides openly selling the book on Amazon (for free), you could offer ½ price sales on the book or a discount if they buy your product.

Even give the book away as a bonus, if they hire you or purchase a minimum amount of product.

The sky is the limit once you have a book.

Depending on which product or service you decide to become affiliated with will depend on how you use a book to your advantage.

Let's suppose you have a software product, and you know all the basics to get the software up and running.

You could do a short 30-page instruction manual or a short explanation on how you use the product. You do not need to own the product to write a book on it.

You do it as an eBook and you create your own cover in Clickdesigns. An excellent design tool that I will be demonstrating online soon.

Using Clickdesigns, I was able to do a markup for this book you are reading.

It looks dynamite. I will be switching to strictly **Clickdesigns** soon.

I try to use as many free tools as possible. It gets to a point where I either love the tool or start looking for a paid tool that will pick up the slack.

With **ClickDesigns** I found an advanced tool that will keep me ecstatic for a long time.

This tool is the perfect complementary tool for Groove and integrates seamlessly.
When this happens, you get the affiliate link for that tool as well.

This is just one way to find a complementary product where you can add to your current niche but make money off of other people's products.

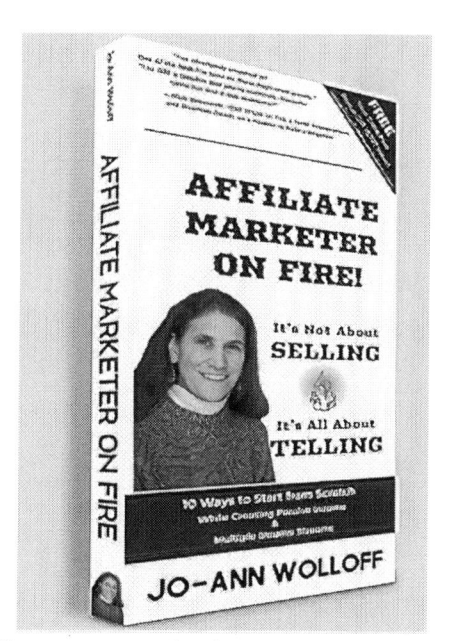

If you want to give it a try yourself, go to:
https://affiliatemarketeronfire.com/clickdesigns

M_a_ny times, these products can actually support your product.

Did you know that Jack Canfield and Kevin Harrington (Shark Tank) are both affiliates for James Malinchak. To the tune of hundreds of thousands of dollars in commissions.

Stop today and think of 10 products you love. Or go back to the first chapter and grab 10 off your list.

Now go and investigate these products or services and see if they have an affiliate program.

It's as easy as going to their websites and looking around or using their 'email us' and asking them if they have an affiliate program.

Or go to GOOGLE and do a search on the product "Does Linktree have an affiliate program" for an example. I used this one because I did this search and got the answer 'No'. Now you know.

But so many other programs that do have one showed up.

No two programs are alike, so please be sure to check the rules of the program and how they pay and when.

All of these things are YOUR RESPONSIBILTY to know. Be an informed affiliate and have fun with it.

Be sure to do it God's Way   Win-Win-Win for everyone.

"You might be an Affiliate If…"
…your house cleaner started a new business called "update home for a week" She will stock the refrigerator, do weekly laundry like having hotel service weekly. You telling anyone?"
Where's your commission?

Ask For Help

That brings us to back to this book.

After I set the launch date for this book, I came down with a bad case of Covid-19.

Luckily the Lord was watching over me and I came through it several weeks later, however I lost a few weeks of time.

Since I am after all an affiliate marketer which means, I am a Connector.

It also meant that I had my seeds sown and I was receiving passive income while I was sick.

Who do I know that would give me some time to help me get back on track in 30 minutes instead of 3 weeks?

Turns out I had an army of people who would step up in a minute to help me out.

Alicia, Deb, Angie, Kathy, Rob and the list goes on, that's the beautiful thing about planting seeds, you have a beautiful garden to pick from…….

Since this was during our Life on Fire Sessions, I reached out to my fire sisters and friends Katie Smith and Jennifer Inniss Eastmond. Without missing a beat, they were there to help me.

So, I would like to give Kudo's to Coach Katie and Jennifer for living in the Image of God always.
Katie has been certified and is a coach/speaker and Best Selling author.

Jenn has always been my tech go to. She's amazing and also has many certifications and has come to my rescue so many times.

I highly recommend not trying to do this alone. Find someone with whom you could form a temporary partnership and do a joint venture.

If you could do them both a solid and check out Katie's YouTube page at:
https://affiliatemarketeronfire.com/coachkatie

Check out Jenn's awesome YouTube channel at:

https://affiliatemarketeronfire.com/jennie (You can thank me later)

Who do you know that you could connect with when you need help? Cherish these relationships, they are not in it for money or glory.

They know God's Way and they live it. Surround yourself with people just like them.

We spend a huge portion of our time helping others.

The more you help others the faster you will get ahead. This is not why you should help others. It is just a fact.

In 2021, I was humbled and honored to received three separate Kingdom Awards, at an Awards Banquet with over 500 of my like-minded friends. In 2022, I received 2 more.

Three of the awards were voted on by my peers. It was like nothing I ever experienced before.

Let's clarify what writing a book could do for you as an affiliate marketer.

Did you like all the Free downloads given away in this book?

That was something I learned recently in one of the 2 challenges. It's called a 'boomerang affect'.

Always, bring them back using the Give First Method.

The benefit the user gets is the FREE Download.

The benefit you get is by having the reader get used to going to your website.

It boomerangs back to you.

The boomerang is beneficial to both parties.

By our putting the links already in the book, no one has to waste time looking them up.

Thanks to James Malinchak for sharing that analogy.
https://affiliatemarketeronfire.com/jamesm

You have so much knowledge that giving away free pdfs or blueprints doesn't hurt and absolutely helps.

As an affiliate (or a human being) you want people to see you as a giver not a taker.

Remember, we have the stigma already attached to the word affiliate. It's up to us to give it a new image.

The Give First Method or God's Way

"You might be an Affiliate If…

…you found a book editor that is quick, efficient and available. All your friends are writing books.

Where's your commission?"

Products or Services

Did you notice how many times I introduced you to the products that I used?

Why would I do that?

If I am being in integrity, it's because those products helped me get ahead.

It's hard to tell someone how you got ahead if you don't tell them what you used to get ahead.

The benefit the user gets is a proven product that has made someone's life easier in the exact niche the user is in.

The benefit you get is, if you are a good affiliate marketer it is your affiliate link for them to get to know the product. It doesn't cost them anymore if you use the company link for your affiliate link.

If they use it, good for them, good for you.

If they don't, then it was not a good fit.

Good for them and good for you.

Every time they hear about that product you will come to their minds.

Did you notice how many of my mentors are in the book?

Did you wonder why? I know, like, trust and have used their services

Up next is a service I actually found while writing this book. It may be one of the best I ever find.

Overwhelm sets In

I ran into an interesting challenge while writing this book.

I knew I wanted to write a book and I also needed to earn an income while writing the book.

But who would do my postings and list building and video editing, email sorting and answering etc....

The answer of course is 'ME or someone else'?

Ideally, I would like to keep control and have someone locally, but that's not feasible and would get very expensive.

The most logical solution would be a Virtual Assistant also known as a VA.

This means someone usually from another country who is skilled in a variety of skills I may not have.

Someone with nothing but time to look after my tasks.

VA's are very inexpensive and are a very common thing these days.

They get hired out on a per task or project basis. Meaning you could use one VA to edit your book and another VA to create a website, another one to set up your database etc.

However, I have never actually used a VA, nor do I know how?

I was actually given 5 hours of access to a VA while I was doing a newsletter and I found it easier to do everything myself because I was clueless on what, when and how to give stuff to a VA.

I really need a secretary type person who will be knowledgeable and invested in what I am doing.

I'm not interested in re-training someone every time I have task to do.

By now you must be asking "What does a VA have to do with affiliate marketing?"

Have you ever wondered how someone comes up with a course or training?

I watched one from scratch recently.

I was at a mastermind weekend and 5 of us were out to supper after the meeting chatting about what we do and what we needed.

Four of us had the exact same complaint.

Not enough time or skill to get things done and no idea how to get and train a VA.

The fifth person already had 2 VA's that she trained from scratch a year ago and are now an intricate part of her success.

Her VAs cut up her video's and make ads or modules for training.

They answer her emails, her blog posts.

They create all her forms and webpages when needed. They do it ALL.

We are still talking VA's here. Very inexpensive way to get things done, but she had the same 2 VAs doing everything.

She interviewed dozens of VA's and gave them tests and tasks until there were only 2 standing.

She purchased the applications they would need to assist her.

Trained them on her brands and preferences till they are now running almost all the projects seamlessly.

We were in awe of her stories and wanted to pick her brain all night.

By the end of the mastermind she stood up and told of new course she was offering. We ignited a fire in her.

She will train on how to submit work to a VA as well as train the VA.

What to expect from our VA.

She will interview dozen of VAs, till she gets the right skill sets of the applications we need for personal business.

All four of us said we were interested.

One week after the class we purchased the newly set up course with a private Facebook page.

She now has a 6 week course set up to train us and our VAs.

She has blueprints and Standard Operating Procedures.

She will instruct us on how to have our VAs create all of our SOPs going forward.

And WAIT FOR IT…… She has an affiliate program.

So lets RECAP:

From one dinner conversation with like-minded people

- There was no course, just conversation.
- There were 4 overwhelmed entrepreneurs with a problem.
- There was an action taker in the group with the skills needed to solve their problem.
- Now a course came into existence and buyers identified as well as an affiliate program set up.

One thing to mention is that the VAs may already be trained on the applications we need.

All 4 of us use GROOVE.

So, she purchased Groove for herself and is now having her VAs transfer all her stuff to Groove. (Saving her tons of money).

This will help them learn Groove before we come on board.

Did you happen to remember that I am a GROOVE affiliate.

That first night we introduced ourselves I was sure to let her know what my product was. (Never knowing the VA idea was even a thought at the time).

As an affiliate you want people to know what your products are otherwise how will they know how you can help them.

Why did I tell you all this?

Would you be interested in one yourself? So many options just became available.

Do you know anyone who would like to free up some time but is clueless on how to do it and doesn't have the time to hire or train a VA?

If you want to find out more go to.
https://affiliatemarketeronfire.com/vatraining

"You might be an Affiliate If..."
---you found a book editor that is quick, efficient and available. All your friends are writing books.

Where's your commission?"

MENTORS

They all went out of their way to service me. If I can show them just a little appreciation, I will every chance I get.

I fully intend to send each of them a signed copy of this book, so they know they are appreciated.

There is always the chance they will show the book to just one person that could make a difference.

If they get students who are interested in affiliate marketing, they may recommend this book.

Remember, I was a student of theirs and that would make me a 'Success Story'.

Proof that what they are teaching really works if you just go into it with the right 'MINDSET' and listen to your mentors

Once you have a Success Story you need to celebrate that.

Good for them, good for me and good for anyone who reads this book and takes away even a couple of golden nuggets they didn't know or that they haven't been practicing.

Maybe you jogged a memory, and they will now TAKE ACTION.

"You might be an Affiliate If…
…you took a Self-Development Class, then you tell everyone you know that they should take it?

Where's your commission?"

MENTIONING OTHERS

Final Tips on how to get started with a book, whether you are the affiliate marketer or have affiliate marketers helping you sell your product.

If I tell you how I got started on the book, it may give you ideas for your niche.

When I started writing this book, I was in a new class with 500 other like-minded people all writing a new book.

- I Posted an introduction in the Facebook Group and watch the post for several weeks.
- I decided to keep everyone accountable weekly with jumping jacks the day of a LESSON
- I declared my launch date for my 'non-existent' book.
- I decided on my title and subtitle (a draft anyway)
- I went to **Clickdesigns** and created a simple markup of the non existent book.
- I created a simple opt-in page in Groove.
- Then I posted a question.
- Who would like to be MENTIONED in my book?
- This was not a promise to put them all in my book.
- This was a 'fishing expedition' to see who is interested.
- I have been diligently figuring that out.
- I was amazed to get over 66 interested applicants.
- Each will be contacted and vetted before possibly getting a mention in one of my next books.
- What these people all have in common is that they are entrepreneurs actively running their businesses.
- They signed up, took action when they saw an opportunity.

- There is a great chance that they have all written a book.
- We could set up a launch party among us and get that each of their books to best seller in one zoom call.
- The possibilities are endless if you open your mind

On the next page I will list all 66 interested parties so far.

This book is the result of the course whose objective was to write a book in 60 Days.

The 60th day is at the end of the week, and I am going to make it! This is the book from that course.

What will happen next is once the dust settles from this book, I will reach out to interested parties and do my research. I will be doing more than 2 books in this series.

NO ONE gets in the book who I have not vetted. Meaning I have to like/love the product/service/book/person.

I have so many more golden nuggets that I found along the way.

You won't find these golden nuggets unless you get started.

It doesn't have to be perfect. As Nick says, "DONE BEATS PERFECT!"

You can start with an idea and watch it grow.

"You might be an Affiliate If…

…you bought a new filter for your pool that saves energy like you've never seen before, and you spread the word.

Where's your commission?"

- Alex Hills
- Alexandria Hernandez
- Allie Rich
- Ana Rutherford
- Angela Alexander
- Angela Wiafe
- Ashriel Walker
- Belle Flowers
- Bruno Melissa
- Calvin Sheppard
- Carla Claibourn
- Chata Ramage
- Cheryl Parris
- Christa Edwards
- Comfort Talabi
- Courtney Fraser
- David Dixon
- Debra Hackney Rieder
- Delxi Fernandez
- Enoch Leffingwell
- Erik & Nora Martinez
- Giselle Johnny
- Grace Oben
- Helen Boateng
- Irene Bryant
- Iva Pace
- Jayne Wambugh
- JD DUNPHY
- Jennifer Inniss Eastmond
- Jennifer Pankratz
- Jessica Elliott
- Jones Sharron
- Joni Killius
- Jose Detre
- Jose Qurioz-Ziebart
- Justin Bell
- Kathi Goodwin
- Kathy Bates
- Kevin Strite
- Lois Morris
- LS Kirkpatrick
- Lucille Shannon
- Lydia Rugh
- Marianne Ambrose
- Marianne van Poortvliet
- Mary Lamborn
- Mary Lou VAIL
- Melanie Johnston
- Melvina Hudson
- Monica Quintero-Devlaeminck
- MYRTHA MILLIEN
- Patrice Brantley
- Paula Jack
- Paulene Gayle
- Pomerleau Danielle
- Rachel White
- Rosemary L. DeJesus
- Sandra Wallace (The OCD Coach)
- Sereda Fowlkes
- Sharon Paratchek
- Sheree Lewis
- Sulena Long
- Tashai Lovington
- Valerie Arbeau
- Veia Hensley
- Virginia Pumulo Roddy
- Wade and Ricquel Ivy
- Win Wolloff (Photographer)

When I sent out the invitation, I was clueless as to what the book was going to be like.

After I got the huge response, I sent out text or emails to 'influencers' and asked if they would be interested in an interview for my book.

Many of them said 'YES' immediately.

I have interviews already set up with:

- James Malinchak
- Angie Norris
- Alycia Lyttle
- CoachDeb
- Cynda Teachman Harris
- Reyna Callejas
- with a few surprise interviews in the mix.

I still intend to ask Jon Talarico, Les Brown (maybe a Tyrone story), Nick & Megan Unsworth, Jack Canfield, Mike Filsaime, Mo Latiff, Kevin Strite, Brian Anderson, David Lemon, Donna fox, Diane Rolston, if you don't ask it is already a NO.

That is another golden nugget. Put out there who you are looking to work with. Someone always knows someone, and they can hook you up.

About the time I started to form my ideas for my book another opportunity showed up and it was directly related to Covid 19, which I happen to have caught that week.

Did you know the government has a REBATE set up for anyone with W2 employees who lost any money during covid or had to shut down?

Did you see me switch topics on a dime? Or did I?

Recently, a friend of mine, got back over $75,000 in rebate money.

This is money paid in income taxes that the government is giving back, because they applied correctly

When he saw what a long-complicated process it was, he turned around and set up a group of people who will do it all for you for a small commission.

Does that sound like affiliate marketing to you? The thing is it's REAL.

Why Choose Recover IRS Rebate?

- Guaranteed To Maximize Refundable Credits For Local And Small To Medium Sized Businesses
- So Easy That Your Entire Commitment Is 15 Minutes
- No Upfront Fees To Get Qualified - 100% Contingent On Your Refund
- Audit-Proof Documentation For IRS Support
- No Other CPA Firm Offers The 15 Minute Refund™

We only specialize in maximizing Employee Retention Tax Credits for small business owners. You won't find us preparing income taxes, compiling financial statements, or providing attestation services of any kind.

When you engage us, rest assured that you've hired the best CPA Firm to lock in this one-time opportunity for a large refund check from the IRS.

If you have or had 5 w2 employees during covid and want to see if you can recover some of that money paid in, there is absolutely no cost to find out: go to https://affiliatemarketeronfire.com/rebate

This affiliate program allows for sub-affiliates where you don't have to buy a thing and be an affiliate for an affiliate. Which means you don't need to learn much either.

See how easy it is to find affiliate deals. I just mention covid and I remembered another opportunity.

My launch date and everyone's schedule are crazy, so I did not push to get everything written in one book.

The decision was made for me. There will be a Series of Affiliate books.

I am looking forward to meeting everyone who asked to be mentioned. You will still need to be 'screened' before you get mentioned in the book.

Remember the first rule of being a great affiliate.

YOU MUST LIKE THE PRODUCT OR SERVICE YOU ARE RECOMMENDING. (that's not negotiable when you are doing it God's Way)

If you have a niche or a product (or even an affiliate marketer who doesn't have their own product) and would like to be considered to be mentioned in a future book it's free go to: https://affiliatemarketeronfire.com/metoo

You will see the following questions.

First	Last Name
Niche/Passion	
Email	
Website or Offer	
Tell me in 200 words or less what you do and who you help.	

"You might be an Affiliate If…

…you got a rebate from your taxes and not everyone even knows it's available.

Where's your commission?"

As an affiliate, keeping in mind that you must know/like/ trust someone and their products in order to even mention them to anyone, I have put together a list of products that I currently promote and love.

Many of these people on my list have started their businesses because of the growing need of new entrepreneurs and others because of the Covid scare.

Some I have seen them start from scratch and I've watched them flourish. Most of them very smartly created Affiliate Programs for their products.

Now you too can make some commissions even if you don't have a product of your own yet.

Full transparency, the links below are my affiliate links to each of them and by using my link it will get you into their products. Some of them have been very generous and are giving away free time, services or products.

Even if you are not interested in the product, if you are an entrepreneur you can learn from their sites. How are they set up? What are they offering?

Keep your eyes open at all times and watch how many products and services you end promoting to people on a daily basis.

WHERE IS YOUR COMMISSION?

You can decide for yourself if you want to apply for their affiliate links yourself and make some money using someone else's products or just model them for your business.

Dave Scatchard - If you haven't read Dave's life story you are missing out. You can buy it on Amazon at **https://bridgingthedigitalgap.com/dave**

It's called "The Comeback.

Dave Scatchard has always been the underdog, but his drive to overcome obstacles meant none of that mattered. That's how his childhood dream of becoming an NHL hockey player came true at twenty-one, followed by marrying the love of his life and starting a beautiful family. For everything that came his way, he always knew he could work hard, fight through the pain, and prove himself.

Everything, that is, until a fifth concussion gave him a taste of death and changed the way he looked at life forever. It took losing it all—his career, his abilities, and very nearly his life—to finally find it all.

Dave's journey through the best and worst of his career to the highs and lows of spiritual and physical healing point to a universal journey we all must take. Just like Dave's life, The Comeback is about far more than hockey.

It's about how we come back to ourselves to find true freedom, weightless abandon, and a pure childlike joy. I

If you would like to know more about how Dave has become a great coach and mentor, periodically he has live events.

The next one is Dec 2,3,4 2022 in Scottsdale AR. It's called
"All-Star Weekend Live Event". As the dates and events change, you can find them at
https://affiliatemarketeronfire.com/dave

Cathy Morenzie - Weight Loss God's Way (WLGW) Cathy is a noted personal trainer, author, blogger and presenter, has been a leader in the health and wellness industry for over 35 years.

Her impact has influenced hundreds of thousands of people over the years to help them lose weight and develop positive attitudes about their bodies, diet and fitness.

Over the years, she has seen some of the most powerful and faith-filled people struggle with their health and their weight. She wondered how it was possible for people to exercise so much power and authority, and yet feel so powerless in the area of health and fitness?

How is it that we have been given the power and authority to cast out demons, yet we can't stop ourselves from eating a piece of chocolate? Why do we struggle with so many issues around our weight such as emotional eating, physical inactivity, self control, guilt and feelings and low-self esteem?

Over the years, Cathy Morenzie– a rational, disciplined, faith-filled, personal trainer struggled with her own weight, with emotional eating, self-doubt and low self-esteem.

She tried to change just about everything about herself for much of her life so she knows what it's like to feel stuck.

Every insecurity, challenge and negative emotion that she experienced was equipping her to help other people who faced the same struggles – especially women.

Want to hear other testimonials and help a loved one break free reach Cathy at **https://affiliatemarketeronfire.com/cathy**

Sandra Wallace - The OCD Coach - Sandra having personal first-hand experience being diagnosed in 1994 with OCD in many forms allows a greater insight.

Do you know anyone with OCD?

Sandra has professional and personal experience with OCD over 28 years.

She can help in designing an individual tailor-made program with and for you.

Did you know that the number one treatment modality cognitive behaviour therapy (CBT) is based on scientific evidence to be effective.

Research shows online therapy is just as effective as one-to-one, face-to-face therapy.

Help out a friend and introduce them to Sandra at

https://affiliatemarketeronfire.com/sandra

Alicia & Lorette Lyttle - Be your own boss and create a freedom lifestyle with your online side hustle working from anywhere, using skills you already have!

I have heard the Lyttle Sisters state that over and over and I am never disappointed. They produce results.

I have watched so many of their students get that jump start they need with their gentle push (if you know Alicia & Lorette, it's not totally gentle) but it is loving and authentic.

They tell it like it is, not what you want them to say. Their honesty is refreshing.

Check out this opportunity at
https://affiliatemarketeronfire.com/lyttle

Deb Cole - Social Video Bootcamp - CoachDeb as her clients affectionally call her since she wrote the 1st book on Twitter back in 2008, has been marketing online since 2001.

CoachDeb has been referred to as "The Digital Gretzky" of online marketing, since she seems to always predict where the puck is going on online marketing since the days she taught Realtors, Realty TV Stars and Entrepreneurs how to get clients using MySpace.

Deborah wrote the Social Media Trilogy Series with all 3 books being the 1st published in the new media marketing space.

In Fact, she wrote about social media before the term was even coined, back in 2006.

Predicting marketing trends and instructing business owners how to get clients and make money using Video Marketing with new tools such as this thing called "YouTube" when its first video was a silly cat video and long before Google bought them.

Her clients are considered first movers and fast action takers who like the advantage of doing what she instructs them first, before their competitors even know what's happening.

She's been working exclusively with high-ticket clients paying her a handsome fee to advise them on the next big thing, giving them the strategic marketing foresight to get that 1st Mover's Advantage.

In Fact, this is the first time she's offering a group coaching program in over a decade! Check her out at
https://affiliatemarketeronfire.com/coachdeb

Kevin Strite - If Groove is the platform you would like to try, here is some help. After signing up for Groove at **https://affiliatemarketeronfire.com/freegroove** you may need some assistance getting started.

Kevin is offering a free guide "Your Best Groove 20 step guide to selling your course with Groove" at: **https://affiliatemarketeronfire.com/kevinguide**

Kevin is the person who kept me up to date when I got too busy to notice Groove updates. He stays on top of all of their changes. Should you still need additional help with Groove, he's your guy.

Because I got into Groove when it was in Beta, they had so many upgrades and changes, it was impossible to keep up, but with Kevin's service it was a no brainer.

If you want to see his main page with many other services including a Free Funnel Build Session go to **https://affiliatemarketeronfire.com/kevinmainpage**

Mo Latif - Mo has created what I like to call Canva on steroids. Clickdesigns is a one-stop-shop. You will never run out of ideas or how to implement them once you start using it.

I love that they have learning videos to get you started. Although, I am new at designing it has already captured my heart and my imagination. To see what I'm talking about go to

https://affiliatemarketeronfire.com/clickdesigns

Angie Norris - When Angie has a promotion you don't want to miss it. She's had such an impact on my life just by watching what she does. She can influence you as well.

See what I mean at **https://affiliatemarketeronfire.com/angie**
(you can thank me later).

Tammy Ossink Doering - The Age Beautifully Coach - If Tammy is an example of what she teaches & sells I don't need more proof.

She looks like she's in her late 30's or early 40's, I'm not letting the cat of the bag but wow she has aged very well.

Do you think she knows something we don't? She makes her own product and it is a huge success. To find out Tammy's secret reach out to her at **https://affiliatemarketeronfire.com/tammy**

Gena Loutsis Peth - Reclaim your family's sanity in a digital world! Life coach - Gena raised 7 teens through the tech (biracial blended family with hers, his, and ours). Gena is offering to help you with your preteens & teenagers manipulate the digital age.

Are You Ready To Learn Screen Time Tech Strategies? Sign up to get access to her FREE Monthly workshops and access to her Calendar for a Free Strategy Call:

https://affiliatemarketeronfire.com/gena

Kate Lemish - She helps busy brides craft gorgeous invitations introducing their guests to what is sure to be the best day ever!

Kate is a graphic designer who helps couples open a window into their upcoming wedding by telling their stories on paper.

Invitations, Save the Dates, Ornaments, Cutting Boards and the list goes on. Make the day special for others too.

If you know of someone with a special occasion coming up, do them a favor and introduce them to Kate. Her work is 10 steps above everyone else Guaranteed.

I am not just saying that because I have been blessed to help raise her as my Bonus daughter.

Reach out to Kate at **https://affiliatemarketingonfire.com/kate**

Parthiv Shah - Parthiv is the founder of a Marketing Agency that serves customers across North America.

Parthiv frequently speaks and attends marketing software industry conventions and small group mastermind sessions where he shares his wealth of marketing knowledge both on stage and in-person.

He invites you to join him on his personal mission and become 1 of the 1000 business owners he will guide in creating at least $100,000 of additional net revenue by December 31, 2025.

If this interests you reach out to Parthiv at:

https://affiliatemarketeronfire.com/parthiv

Win Wolloff - Photography or prints   If you are looking for something special, a headshot or christmas card or a family photo and you are local to the Tampa Bay, Florida area you are in luck, be sure to look up Win.

If you are not local jump onto his website and see the incredible photography prints he has to offer. Would make incredible gifts for people you love. Win has been a photographer for over 50 years and he changed with the times coming into the Digitial world with everyone else.

His many accomplishments include 2022 President of TAPPA (Tampa's Photography Organization).

His biggest accomplishment would be as my loving husband, the father to our children and grampy to our grandkids.

You can find Win at: **https://affiliatemarketeronfire.com/win**

As I finish this book, I have one more proposition to throw out there. Have you ever been in an MLM that is worth being a part of?

When I was smaller the MLM, I remember the most was called "Amway". My mom and some friends dabbled in it, but I never really understood them.

They have changed a lot and now I know so many people doing them that I thought I should investigate it a bit.

I still don't know a lot about it, however, here's what I did learn about this one that I was approached to participate in. There are 2 legs, and you get paid once the legs are even.

I have a sponsor who was going to help me build one of my legs and I am to build the other. Not having a clue what that meant I joined and as I so often did back them, I put it on the shelf while paying my monthly minimum to stay active.

Well, here we are 7 months later and on her leg of the deal I see over thousands of people have signed at some point on this one leg. (I believe just under 1,000 active).

As I said I am still learning what all this means. I think I dropped the ball here. All I have to do is build the other leg to start getting paid.

With everything I am doing I will not have the time to properly train and learn the business, however, I know a great thing when I see one, so I want to take this off the shelf.

So here's my question. Is there anyone reading this book who has experience in MLM or has a huge following where we could explore growing this leg together and make it a joint venture?

I realize this is not a lot of info, but I really didn't want to be promoting the product here. I wanted to promote a Joint Venture. Notice in this book how many ways there are to get passive income.

How many ways have you learned to reach out with an opportunity. If you don't tell someone, no one will know what you are doing.

If you are interested for more info or possibly a joint venture reach out to me   https://affiliatemarketeronfire.com/mlm

Final word on MINDSET

Do not add pressure to yourself.

It is great to 'stretch your limits' but know there are limits.

You should always be challenging yourself to grow.

Just know your limits, try to keep the overwhelm down when you can.

Your health must always be put first in front of your ambition.

Several incredible opportunities came up this month while I was writing this book.

I will tell you in my next book this summer.

If you learned anything about Affiliate Marketing from this book, I hope it is to **Tell not Sell** and **always deal in integrity.**

If it's not a Win – Win   -   walk away.

Adopt the

"NO ONE LEFT BEHIND"

Scenario

This is my favorite Scripture: Romans 12:5-10 GNBUK

In the same way, though we are many, we are one body in union with Christ, and we are all joined to each other as different parts of one body.

So, we are to use our different gifts in accordance with the grace that God has given us. If our gift is to speak God's message, we should do it according to the faith that we have; if it is to serve, we should serve; if it is to teach, we should teach; if it is to encourage others, we should do so.

Whoever shares with others should do it generously; whoever has authority should work hard; whoever shows kindness to others should do it cheerfully. Love must be completely sincere.

"You might be an Affiliate If...
...you are one of us who believes in GOD
&
You can't wait to tell someone how Great He
is. **His LOVE is our Commission!"**

Pastor Dan   Pastor Michael   Pastor Corey
We have many Pastors, we love to have fun, join us if you can.

ONE LAST MESSAGE!

In Service recently, (Journey Church Tampa), I heard Pastor Michael, telling about Authority.

I had already picked out this scripture that reads whoever has authority should work hard.

Then Pastor Cheryl talked about a course she just finished about the Good Hard or is it the Hard Good?

I was intrigued and will dive into it in the next book of the Series.

Today's Service was wonderful as well. I want to share some quotes from Patrick Morley

"If you want to lead a balanced life, decide how many hours you want to work and stick to your guns."

"Put **work** appointments on your calendar **in pencil** but put your **family commitments in pen.** "

"**Love is time and Time is love.**"

The whole world has clues on how to be an affiliate and it all points to the Give First Model – God's Way.

For those of you who can't get out to your church and would like to join a service online, we meet every Sunday morning. 10:30 est. Or if you would like to hear more from our Pastors you can visit.
https://journeychurchtampa.com

Should you take a vacation to Fl and are near

Tampa/Riverview area we'd love for you to join us.

Acknowledgments

Through the years, many have shared ideas, mentoring and support that has impacted my life, each in a different way. It's impossible to thank everyone and I apologize for anyone not listed. I appreciate you greatly. (No particular order)

God, Terry & Ray Thivierge, Win Wolloff, Kate Lemish, Corey Wolloff, Jami Wolloff, Jeanne Martell, Lauren DeLorie, Andrea Wolloff, Jay Lemish, Jenn Wolloff, Pastor Dan & Val Farr, Jeanne Cormier, George Antone, Angie Norris, Bob & Brenda Loder, Alicia Lyttle, Deb Cole, Reyna Callejas, Annette Lavallee, Blanche & Herve Thivierge, Raymond Thivierge, Cynda Teachman Harris, Maryanna & Andy Papadopoulos, John DeLorie, Jocelyn Thivierge, DJ Brown, Katie Smith, Joe Jablonski, Megan Unsworth, Robbie & Bob Chamberland, Tony Robbins, Jon Talarico, Lorette Lyttle, Reagan Wolloff, Les Brown, Nick Unsworth, Rick & Rhonda Mathena, Colby Lemish, James Malinchak, Deb & Lee Wolloff, Russell Thivierge, Kathy Walls, Deb Noury Hershberger, Warren & Mary Wolloff, Richard & Randi Sanford, Tony & Linda Marcelli, Carrie Watson, Daniel Michaels, Richard Thivierge, Deb Dufault Marceau, Robert Thivierge, Maverick Wolloff, Judy & Roland Gosselin, Donna Fox, Dianne Morin, Joe Horton, Jan & Jim O'Malley, Phil Bisaga, Brenda Wehrly, Rosanne Hayden, David Lemon, Tim Parker, Keith Gaspers, Nancy & Bill Doyle, Tiffany Vitale, Kaitlyn Hyatt, Monchel Sharp, Sue Riendeau, Cil Cote, Al Martell, Rebecca Wilcox, Jennifer Inniss Eastmond, Kevin Strite, Ron Thivierge, Dick & Barbara Lemish, Brian Anderson, Brenda Compton Lech, Rachel Thivierge, Nancy Picard, Mike & Michelle Filsaime, Pastors Val & Michael Kyker, Dawn & Leo Cote, Cindy McLane, Jackie Guernon St.Jean, John Pellizzari, Sereda Fowlkes, Debra Rieder, Irma Matos, Donald & Deb Scarboro, Rob Verzera, Chuck & Pat Vosburgh, Mari Jaworsky, Andi Anderson, Austin Barnes, Thelma Noury, Ann Joe,

Javier Zayas, Pastor Pete & Rose Soden, Melanie Johnston, Joni Killius, Maureen & Cam Fagnant, Pete & Del Morin, Peggy Gossage, Lenny Hanson, Pat Mckie, Terri Drews, Tommy Poland, Marissa Smith, Geff Oakley, Andy & Ralph Kumlin, Iva Lozina, Victoria Walker, Joe & Violet Detre, Jim & Tammy Doering, Shirley & Roger Dufault, Nancy & Dan Feely, Irene & Marty Wallach, Teri & Mike Magnan, Cubby & Mitch Gravel, Michelle Ducharme Brodeur, Jack Canfield, Mark Lepinski, Trish & Tina Tessier, Donna Maurice, Caro Savino, Diane Rolston,

-THE NEXT GENERATION: Elissa & Jay, Adam & Keri, Joshua W, Gabe, Dawn, Joy, Jill & John, Rob & Andi, Joe B, Travis, Trevor, Maura, Faith & Tim, Jaymie, Stephanie, Joshua T & Jodi, Joe Thivierge, Jaymie, Michael & Chaney, Steven & Brittany, Brenda & Isacc, Tyson, Shaunna, Johnny, Chris, Aiden & Reilly Unsworth, Jayden, Reilly & Chase and Adeline.

ABOUT JO-ANN

Jo-Ann Wolloff's online career may just be a few years old, but her IT experience stems almost 40 years and she's taking her online career an shooting off like a rocket.

Jo-Ann is an International Speaker/Coach. She has shared the stage with Jack Canfield, James Malinchak, Joe Theismann, Nick Unsworth, Megan Unsworth, Lakiesha Michelle, Pastor Keith Kraft, Steve Weatherford,

Jo-Ann was asked to participate in several Inspirational Panels with no notice and recently received this glowing review from Nick Unsworth **"You absolutely smashed it! One of the Best I've seen on these Inspiration Panels"**. **"You ARE a Speaker and your authentic character came out and it was awesome!"**

Jo-Ann is recognized in Life on Fire as the "glue that keeps LOF going" according to Nick Unsworth's Facebook Post recently. Jo-Ann has received Five Kingdom Awards, For the Most Successful & the Most Helpful in both 2021 & 2022. Also, the 5 & 6 Figure Awards. Jo-Ann made over 5 figures in 4 different months during 2021.

Jo-Ann is friends with people like James Malinchak from the TV ABC's Hit series "Secret Millionaire". He recently stated **"If you're ready to positively transform your life, then read and absorb the strategies in this brilliant book by my friend JoAnn Wolloff! She truly cares about helping others and her ideas will make a positive difference in your life!"**

Jo-Ann has raised over $140,000 for one product in record time. She's a best selling author and she's just getting started. Jo-Ann is a #1 Best Selling Author and she is just getting started.

Jo-Ann does things God's Way

https://bridgingthedigitalgap.com

When God blesses you financially,

don't raise your standard of living. Raise your standard of giving.